Martin Lux
ANTI-FASCIST

ANTI-FASCIST

MARTIN LUX

Phoenix Press
London
2006

Published in 2006 by
Phoenix Press
PO Box 824
London
N1 9DL

Copyright © Phoenix Press and Martin Lux

ISBN 0-948984-35-X

Cover illustrations by Laura Norder
Design and DTP by Jayne Clementson

Printed and bound in the UK by Polestar Wheatons, Exeter

*Many thanks to Laura and Anthony
for helping me render this work
into readable English.*

CHAPTER 1

I guess my anti-racism was partly a reaction to my background: a background from which I'd sought escape for almost as long as I can remember. In the recesses of my fertile imagination I'd always harboured dreams of a bohemian lifestyle. For sure, I wanted nothing to do with moronic, boring football, the number one obsession of my doomed contemporaries. And anyhow, as something of a raspberry ripple, I was hardly destined for success in the beautiful game.

Home life only fuelled these dreams of escape: drunken Paddy father constantly fulminating against 'fookin darkies'; rows leading to punch-ups erupting all too sporadically. As for fascism, I thought, "fuck that shit!" I was a natural born anarchist, hating and despising authority, working-class conservatism and all it's manifestations. I wanted shot of that dull scene, pronto, but was hemmed in on all sides: socially, economically and educationally. It would prove difficult to break out. And escape into what? I wanted to fight the prevailing ethos, both verbally and physically. And fighting – slugging it out, win or lose – is just what you did in such a crap environment, like it or not. Aged sixteen, just starting work, and by then somewhat beefy I was up for it big style, limpy leg notwithstanding.

Come my seventeenth birthday, January 1970, I'd still never really done anything 'political'. I was vaguely aware of radical and revolutionary ideas, mainly down to my being an avid reader of the underground and alternative press, my first real lifeline. I devoured such publications as *Oz* and *IT*. I'd also taken to visiting Speakers' Corner of a Sunday afternoon, and enjoyed finding myself embroiled in the numerous discussions and more heated debates there. These experiences on top of my natural inclinations led me towards an increasing loathing of authority, religion and any such garbage by the week. Being young though, I also spent plenty of time getting off my nut, going to music gigs, having the odd bit of horizontal entertainment and vanishing from the happy home for days on end. Naturally, as was the anti-fashion of the wannabe bohemian young I dressed rather informally. None of that Mohair-Crombie bollocks, you'll-never-get-a-bird-unless-you-wear-a-suit shite for me. What did they know? I had better things to spend my hard-earned on. Drugs and booze for one. As a concession to the mean streets I wore steel-toed footwear: order of the day if I was going to protect myself against the marauding boneheads who always enjoyed giving some 'long 'aired hippy cunt' a good kicking.

After one particularly blinding, drug-fuelled couple of days as I stumbled along Holloway Road towards the parents' gaff, I spied through the haze a crowd gathered in front of the Nag's Head pub. Curious as ever, I soon discovered that a 'Nazi' group, the National Front, were inside. Those outside were planning some sort of meet-and-greet reception to follow their meeting. So despite my frazzled state, I hung around to see what ensued. There was plenty of animated debate not unlike Speakers' Corner, the emphasis being on 'immigration'. The most vociferous opponents of racism and of Enoch Powell were a group of Irish trade-unionists, bus workers from the nearby garage. This made a welcome change from the rancid Paddies I'd endured over the years; ignorant racists endlessly cursing the 'fooking niggers' and 'paki coonts'. I weighed in on the side of the anti-racists, arguing that Enoch Powell was a Tory bastard, an upper class cunt. Some middle aged Alf Garnett thickheads countered this with the usual shite about Powell 'speaking for the working man'. Sick to the stomach with this puke-inducing refrain, encountered with great regularity in the work-place and at home, I stepped in again only to be told, "Get your fuckin hair cut, son." The previous days' excesses had done little to improve my temper and soon we were trading insults galore to the amusement of an ever-growing crowd.

Then, sudden pandemonium. The Front emerged from their watering hole. I'd half expected geezers togged up in Nazi uniforms, swastika armbands, or at least some blackshirt gear. What slid forth instead was a right sad-looking bunch. Child molestor types, in ill-fitting suits replete with the odour of faded mothballs, escorted by hard nuts with short-back-and-sides barnets and tight leather jackets, and it was only moments before fighting erupted, bottles smashing above the heads of the fascists. A general brawl ensued, whilst I exited swiftly before the meat wagons arrived. No point in me hanging about – unfit for rucking, dope stashed about my person.

The Front stood a candidate in the constituency for that year's General Election. But I wasn't active in that locale, concentrating my disruptive efforts elsewhere. There wasn't much going down anyhow. Apart from the Holloway punch-up, no opposition. My only local activity was to deface or tear down their posters. One minor confrontation resulted from my ripping down a Front poster outside my house. Suddenly some angry old fart was crossing the street to remonstrate. Before he'd even reached my side the old bastard was yelling, howling something about getting a job. I yanked out my pay packet to confound him with proof positive. But my employment status was not the issue any more. Now he launched into the familiar repertoire: joining the army, Enoch Powell ... the usual bollocks. My attempting to explain to him that the NF were nazis – worshippers of the same goose-stepping creed he no doubt fought against in the war – cut no ice. He simply blustered off advising me to 'get a bloody haircut'. Lucky for him I wasn't in too bad a mood or I might have lost it and given the old cunt a well deserved smack in the puss. Instead I was mellow, having just smoked a nice fat joint.

CHAPTER 2

The closest thing I got to an education from 1969 onwards was my weekly stroll down Speakers' Corner. Here a fascinating collection of speakers including communists, racists, anarchists and black-power firebrands lined up alongside atheists, pranksters, and religious nuts to provide the masses with free entertainment. A meagre smattering of wit and repartee aside however, few speakers had material or imagination enough to interest us more than once: cranks as most inevitably were, they quickly tended towards the repetitive. We gave them short shrift, shouting them down with the much-heard refrains: "We've heard that tune before," "Turn the record over," "Play us the other side."

It was in the arguments, discussions and general argy on the fringes that the real education was to be had. As a result of both intensive reading and these hours-long discussions, I was soon well able to hold my own on the street. Of course this was difficult at first as some of these folks had had years of experience shooting the breeze, but I soon got into the flow. I'd never mastered a foreign tongue, but soon I was fluent in dialectical materialism plus all the various grades of Communist, Maoist and Trotskyite blurb. And of course, Anarchism. Being influenced by hedonistic alternative culture, and in particular the underground press, I brought a new angle to these chin-wags: a feistily street-level, class analysis of society blended with a heady mixture of direct action, revolution, sex, drugs and rock 'n' roll. And aggro. Plenty of it. I found the leftists somewhat socially conservative. They were rarely impressed with the sex 'n' drugs: "It's easy to shock the bourgeoisie, but rather more difficult to overthrow them Mart, old son." Quite bizarrely, they claimed that homosexuality was a product of decadence that would 'wither away' under socialism – "It's a dysfunction of the bourgeois lifestyle. They pick it up at public school" – all patent nonsense, which in the tortuous jargon of the dialectically inclined can be refuted at a stroke through 'empirical observation'. A couple of gay Maoists insisted that 'Gay Communes' existed in China – wishful thinking on a par with the spoutings of holy rollers – to which I retorted, "A strange name for concentration camps!"

If there was anything on which we all agreed, it was anti-racism. This led us into many rows bordering on fisticuffs with the various racists and fascists who turned up to peddle their ideological wares. Here I was on firm ground, waxing sarcastic, attempting to subvert their idiocy. Enoch Powell was their hero. It was disturbing, nauseating to hear working-class people spout this reactionary crap. But at least I could now have a proper go at them.

For me the main attraction of the lefties was their participation in political aggro against the system, especially against the old bill. As this miserable conformist island had sidestepped the world-shaking events of 1968, I felt I'd been cheated. I desperately wanted hardcore action. Demonstrations were alright for the odd punch-up or two. But I was after full-on riot, looting, burning, occupations, barricades, insurrection: the whole revolutionary head-rush. Better than football any day. My own belief at the time was that the much-touted 'vanguard', the students, were a bunch of tossers, more frightened of the lower-orders than the state. I was equally damning of the conservative working class most of whom in my fierce impatience I regarded as racist scum grovelling at the feet of the foreman. I saw no evidence that they were willing or able to take on capitalism, to 'fulfil their historic role'. My hopes were pinned on the marginal young, extreme fringes, counter culture, disaffected blacks, along with anyone or group that had had enough of stifling conformity, crap existence, exploitation and the general arrogance of those who ruled their lives. Everything seems possible when you're seventeen.

CHAPTER 3

Speakers' Corner then, was a combination of hothouse and nuthouse and naturally attracted all varieties of nazi, fascist and racist. Any speaker of this loathsome brand got a well-deserved barracking. It didn't take long for me to roll up my sleeves and get involved in lengthy arguments with rabid anti-semites and National Front members. I had a slight advantage, if one could call it that, since I was an avid reader of their literature – difficult in fact to obtain, until I discovered a newsagent in Fleet Street who dealt it under the counter, just like one-armed literature. I recall the NF magazine Spearhead. Whilst not exactly hardcore in its language it certainly sailed close to the wind. The keyword, 'Jew' was hardly mentioned. In its place were various euphemisms: 'Zionists', 'Cosmopolitans', 'One-Worlders', 'International Financiers', 'the Ubiquitous One Percent', 'a people whose origin is far removed from that of the Anglo-Saxon yeomen and bowmen'. Reading this stuff, which in layout and presentation reminded me of old-fashioned hobby publications, didn't alter my opinions one iota. It did, however, make me realise that their anti-immigrant, anti-black propaganda was merely sucker-bait intended to lead mugs to a realisation of their 'real' enemy: those eternally plotting 'Learned Elders', the Jews. Of course they still hated blacks, 'pakis', whatever, it goes without saying.

I didn't become 'corrupted' through reading this stuff though, not seeing anything of the remotest value in it, aside from its allowing me an insight into what they thought. In fact I soon developed a degree of cynicism in my dealings with these creeps: nevertheless, at least I could now talk with them in their own terminology, or converse in Chimpanzee as Doctor Doolittle would have it. And creeps they were; typical grubby anoraks, emotional cripples, sexually repressed... They were hardly the fine physical specimens of manhood they imagined themselves to be. And flesh and blood examples of the valkerian maidens that adorned their shoddy publications were even thinner on the ground.

The lefties generally didn't bother themselves with locking horns with the Master Race, regarding them as beneath contempt. This left the field open to a combination of blacks, Jews, Zionists, Irish and young anarchist troublemakers. Naturally, we all did as much as possible to wind up the übermenschen. After all, how can you engage in serious debate with morons who believe in a Jewish conspiracy to dominate the world, to mongrelise the white race or to deny the extermination of the six million? ('Holocaust' wasn't common currency in those days). Most embarrassing for the nazis was the unhappy fact that they had little or no knowledge of England's history, evolution, development, its culture or literature. Instead, they decried communism, sexual permissiveness, drugs, immigration, race-mixing... "Yeah mate, that's one thing I'd agree with you on. Flat and National Hunt shouldn't be on the same card."

"Typical gullible Goy, giving your money to the Jewish bookmaker." Such was the stunning level of their repartee.

They praised authority, discipline, 'Britishness', capital punishment, so us sarky young reprobates had a field day: taking the piss, ridiculing them personally, and ripping their ideology apart. The situation occasionally overheated, and punches were thrown. One of their more infuriating tactics in these encounters was their sarcastic and selective use of euphemisms. No 'niggers', 'coons', 'pakis' or 'sambos' for them: instead they used terms such as 'Our Coloured Brethren' or 'Your Commonwealth Cousins', all delivered in mock-unctuous tones. Sometimes they'd let slip the odd 'darkie' or 'blackie'. But when it came to the 'real' enemy, the 'Cosmopolitan', 'Zionist' stuff was all shelved for the purpose of such confrontations, as their favourite word, 'Jew', pronounced a slurred 'Dew', was spat from thin lips dripping with venom. And when sufficiently riled, all inhibitions disappeared; 'yids', 'shonks' and other choice morsels rang out loud and clear. Most of these episodes were terminated with fists, as tempers and passions frayed.

But at least the nazis made no attempt to convert us hippies and degenerates: probably hoping to draw sympathy from onlookers or listeners. Fat chance. A less inspiring collection of human flotsam would be difficult to imagine. Many seemed to be fairly old, whilst the younger of the species had a distinct air of the cat-strangler about them. They only really came to life with anything like proselytising zeal if a gang of skinheads turned up. Here, they believed were potential stormtroopers. But even then it usually went badly for the übers, with the skins joining the merriment on our side.

When not being drawn by us, however, the nazis' and racists' main topic of conversation was Enoch Powell, who'd inadvertently helped to put them back on the map. He'd certainly opened the field to them to propagate their racism by making anti-black and anti-asian rhetoric common currency. And such was the sick state of British society that so long as they kept within these parameters they retained in Joe Punter's eyes at least, a veneer of respectability. In other words it was okay to hate blacks or 'coloured immigrants', but Jews were the great unmentionable, except for when we drew it out of them. The Powellite garbage was the only real subject they could milk and they played it for all it was worth.

As the months passed in the warm summer of 1970 and beyond things became more acrimonious. Admittedly things had hardly started as a love-in. They were always quick with the usual, "Get your hair cut," "Get a job." But as you'd get plenty of that from Alfs in the street, parents and workmates it didn't have much effect. But when they started calling us 'Jew lovers', 'dupes' or even Jews, they'd crossed the line. We'd respond with a "Thanks for the compliment Adolf." Sometimes when they'd get really personal we'd respond with like. Not that I really minded being called 'Shonky boy' but when I retaliated, fists flew instantly, a general mêlée ensuing. Another time I casually remarked to one idiot, "I'm tired of hearing you go on about queers, bumboys and homos when we all know you'd love to be dragged into a cubicle by a nice limp-wristed college boy." This earned me an instant smack in the chops, added to which was the indignity of being marched out of the park by the police. Freud would have found an endless seam of raw material amongst that crowd of nazi closet-cases.

Some of the worst racists and anti-semites weren't even the paid-up nazis, but people just passing through or regulars. A few in particular spring to mind: a couple of elderly Irish women who could only be described as revolting old hags, smothered in ill-applied makeup, rendering their lips cruel slashes. They wouldn't have been out of place in the opening scenes of the Scottish Play. And never have I before or since met two people so thoroughly obsessed with the Jews: I'd say that they'd long passed the point of insanity. They were so repulsive, such an assault on the eyes – and with their hideous shrieking, the ears too – that I couldn't bear arguing with them, let alone looking at them. But this didn't stop them following me around the park hurling their abuse, "Jewboy lover," amongst their favourite epithets. Worse still were a couple of middle-aged thugs built like brick shithouses, who, in the company of giggling spouses of long-faded attraction, embarrassed even the nazis. Their favourite routine was to pull out a coin: "Here's a shilling for Hitler's meter!" And whenever the magic word 'Jew' was uttered one of the women would howl "Up the chimneys wiv 'em!" It didn't take a month of Sundays before we lost patience with these brutes, and after a couple of violent scraps they learned to take their weekly constitutional elsewhere.

I found myself, not unwillingly, sucked into all this aggro. I was friendly with some hardnut Zionists I knew from various adventures around the dog-tracks and dives of Hackney. This did little to endear some of the lefties to me, but it was my life: I did as I pleased, hung out with whoever amused me. During one heated bout of argy-bargy that spilled beyond the park railings, I lost my cool, chinning an über who'd gobbed in my face. A lucky smack, it sent him flying into a refreshment stall, Pepsis, Cokes, ice cubes scattering. As I turned to face off his racial comrades a blow to the side of my head caused me to lose balance, crashing down the steep stone stairs past bewildered tourists. As I lay stunned, brawling erupted all around me, my only view of proceedings being boots and shoes cutting through the air.

I'd cracked a bone in my knee and had to spend a fortnight off work in great pain.

In my absence production soared and I got the sack. From that time on, dialogue was suspended. The nazis were always squaring-up for a fight – some perceived insult leading to a deadly threat – and they were usually first out of the traps when it came to a knuckle. After a couple more brawls they gave up coming to the park. But I'd had enough contact with then to utterly loath and despise the fuckers. Some of the violence, as opposed to the propaganda, had rubbed off. If they ever took to the streets big-style, I for one would be there with my steelies itching and a half brick in my pocket. And I wouldn't be pleased to see them.

CHAPTER 4

A boiling hot Sunday, another day at the park. But today was something special as an anti-racist march was leaving for Downing Street. Others had alternative plans. By coincidence the ultra right-wing Monday Club were holding an anti-Common Market rally in nearby Trafalgar Square. The grapevine had it that the National Front were turning up to lend support to their fellow xenophobes. Could be fun. Thousands gathered at the Speakers' Corner rendezvous, including a scattering of boneheads who were overwhelmed by the anti-racists. Us park regulars argued with them, me especially since I'd recently emerged from an identically miserable educational background and was about the same age as the older ones. The poor skins were verbally slaughtered, surprised that white geezers were arguing against racism and the tin god Enoch. Apart from a couple of nasty, vicious bastards of a psycho stripe, the rest weren't bad lads really. They just wanted a laugh. A couple showed interest in the forthcoming anti-Vietnam war demo, "It'll be a massive ruck with the Old Bill." It was this sentiment rather than Historical Materialism that would be more interesting. And it was certainly so with me.

The march, after the customary hour's wait, finally set off. It seemed to be dominated by Asians. And why not? They'd endured enough of the 'paki-bashing' craze and all sorts of foul abuse from the Enoch-lovers. I stuck with the anarchist types and the Speakers' Corner mob, all in fine spirits as the odd joint circulated chanting, "DISEMBOWEL EUNUCH POWELL!" zonked out of our nuts. After the usual stop, start eternity we arrived at Downing Street for the delivery of a petition. We weren't interested in that minor detail, heading instead straight up Whitehall to the Square. Tons of police, sweaty under the collar, were on duty. Obviously they'd foreseen trouble but failed to prevent opposing knots of agitated people shouting insults at each other. Then, down a side street, confrontation: about a hundred of us ran into a group of right-wingers of about the same number. They were looking for the same thing as us – trouble – and they got it. Only a handful of police were struggling in vain to separate the two sides as we laid into each other with gusto, belting each other with four-by-twos. The right were that curious blend of seedy middle-aged sex-offender types garbed in faded Sunday-bests, hardnuts in leather jackets and massive skinheads with sideburns, gleaming scalps and steel-capped cherry-reds. I caught a glancing blow to the noggin, drawing blood, and retaliated with a heavy lashing kick from my own steelies, landing a crunching blow to a leather jacket's knee. I never had the pleasure of seeing him hit the deck, if indeed he did, however because police reinforcements rushed in to break up the sideshow.

My wound was superficial so I headed back to the Square. The place was brimming with Front rather than Monday Clubbers although the latter had produced an amusing placard with the slogan 'RED JACKBOOTS FOLLOW STUDENT CHATTER'. I'd been smacked with one of these. Due to the presence of large number of constabulary we merely amused ourselves with an exchange of insults. Nothing sophisticated, merely the usual, "Long 'aired red Commie scum," versus, "Fascist pigs." Exciting as this might have been for a moment or two, we soon tired of it, setting off instead for the American Embassy where some yanks were planning to burn their draft cards. Following this well-attended event we drifted off to the usual watering hole for a couple of swift halfs. Then I nipped down Portobello Road to score a quid deal before a late date. Exhausted from a day's manic activity I took Monday off. Again.

CHAPTER 5

The nearest thing to mass fascism I got to see in the early seventies wasn't a bunch of Union Jack or swastika waving numbskulls, it was something far more insidious, operating on the social-sexual level: the bizarrely named Festival of Light. The repulsive Mary Whitehouse, Lord Longford and Malcolm Muggeridge and a gruesome collection of right-wing Christian Fundamentalists were the mainstays. They rallied against sexual permissiveness, pornography, gay liberation, the alternative press, abortion, devilry and of course, drugs. Normally such rubbish as the Festival of Shite could have been dismissed with a bemused shrug, but they succeeded where we'd failed miserably. They'd created, if only temporarily, a mass movement of the young. The whole shebang was cobbled together by the churches – both mainstream and evangelical – youth groups and religious nightclubs; and naturally it lacked any spontaneity bar the inevitable outpourings of the pent-up sexual energies of its participants. A top-down hierarchical outfit, whose summit consisted solely of aged right-wing dinosaurs, it had nevertheless mobilised tens of thousands of working- and lower middle-class young of both genders. The left, regardless of the obvious political agenda being paraded under their very noses, were remarkably silent. This was probably due to their own worship of an anally retentive vision of the proletariat: the lantern-jawed, rigid archetypes of socialist realism. The left itself in most of its shapes and forms was sexually and socially conservative with a marked lack of comprehension, if not downright hostility when it came to the 'decadent' underground press, sex, drugs and hedonism in general.

I, however, had a multitude of reasons for my profound hostility. I'd verbally clashed with all manner of Christian religious nut every Sunday afternoon. I was also well aware of growing police and government repression of the underground press. Not to mention harassment of every public manifestation of the alternative lifestyle from free festivals, down to informal gatherings on the streets of a summer night around our favoured haunts of Ladbroke Grove and Portobello.

The FOL may not have been red-clawed fascism but its political and social agenda was certainly ultra-conservative. The religious element wasn't exactly Liberation Theology either. Like fascism, the FOL had mobilised sections of the oppressed against their own interests, banging the drums of obedience, deference to authority and sexual fear. The FOL held mass rallies that were imaginatively disrupted by subversives. Gay liberationists took the initiative, with one notable incident at a central London rally where the platform was rushed by a group of transvestite bearded nuns. In an unofficial capacity many Front heavies moonlighted as stewards, neatly tying the FOL in with real fascism.

After a summer of successful counter-actions the FOL announced an October demonstration against 'MORAL POLLUTION', the catchy slogan being, 'THERE IS ONLY ONE SOLUTION TO MORAL POLLUTION'. It had without the slightest irony, the ring of another, final, solution; but the secret desires of the NF stewards aside, the 'solution' in question was meant to involve some hairy geezer who got himself nailed to a tree two thousand years ago.

On the appointed Saturday, the FOL were to march from Trafalgar Square to Hyde Park where they'd be treated to a concert featuring bible-bashing luminaries, with Cliff Richard the star turn. Groovy. For months I visited every malcontent troublemaker, anarchist, joker and miscreant I knew urging them to disrupt, subvert and oppose the event. Women's and gay liberationists, plus those in the alternative scene were also organising for the day. All were of the mind that direct action combined with a generous dollop of piss-taking and a carnivalistic display would be preferable to some boring counter-demo. We wanted fun.

I arrived in Trafalgar Square early to banter with the credulous, proclaiming myself to all who would listen a fire-breathing Calathumpian. It had the desired effect and I was revelling in the effect, as the faithful shot me the sort of looks I'd have thought were reserved for the devil incarnate. Four morons in particular afforded me the dubious pleasure of having them fall to their knees before me, to pray earnestly for my lost soul. Dragging myself away from this distraction, I joined Lucifer's flock. And although our usual combination of unkempt hair, urban guerrilla chic and degenerate hippie gear would have been sufficient to induce apoplexy amongst 'the saved' on an ordinary day, many had donned fancy dress for the occasion, with bearded nuns once again in abundance. The vast majority of the FOL crowd were youngsters with skin problems, clothed in the heights of trainspotting fashion. Collected from church, youth and evangelical organisations, mostly from the provinces, they appeared glassy-eyed, overawed by the Big Smoke perhaps – or was this their usual blissed-out-on-Jesus look? Alarmingly, though, they were tens of thousands strong.

Hurling sardonic comment, abuse and the odd vegetable harvested from nearby Covent Garden market, we dogged them as they proceeded to their destination. Admittedly it was all great fun for us as the police were thin on the ground. Some may have been off-duty acting as stewards, as there were some burly bastards in that role standing in stark contrast with the puny youth they shepherded. No surprise either to see known Fronters tending the flocks.

Arriving at Hyde Park, after a few adventures, we linked up with the main body of the opposition all intent on causing mischief, mayhem and disruption. Some of the more determined had been waiting at the foot of the concert stage, bags loaded with rotten groceries and smoke bombs tucked in coats. I personally was hell bent on more immediate fun and games. We harassed the stiffs. Some kids in family groups were shielded from visual contact. Truly, we were the people their parents had warned them against as some of our banners proudly proclaimed. Soon we were scuffling with police, stewards and religious cranks some of whom were in a state of extreme hysteria. Recognised by an irate, truncheon swinging police sergeant who we'd decked the previous month on a Ladbroke Grove pavement, I was chased deep into the ranks of bleating Christians. Safe but isolated, I felt vulnerable as the levels of general hysteria reached a disturbing pitch. This was a mixture of bad trip and a Christian Nuremberg. It came as blessed relief to be reunited with the devil's spawn, having elbowed my way through Jesus Freaks waving their mitts in the air by the thousand as they chanted the name of their saviour.

For hours, until the chill of late afternoon drew in we argued and took the piss big style, putting on a comic display of 'degeneracy'. We must have numbered a thousand with even some of the crusty lefties seeing the light and turning up for the entertainment. After all, the FOL had tied 'MORAL POLLUTION' to 'COMMUNIST SUBVERSION', despite most communists being just as stiff and repressed as our religious brethren. As the rally approached its anti-orgasmic climax, some of us made our way to the side of the stage hoping to witness the bombardment of Saint Cliff. Sure enough fruit, veg and eggs flew in abundance, many hitting the target. A besplattered Cliff didn't seem best pleased. Fights broke out up front. I didn't fancy climbing back into that particular cauldron as things were getting very heavy. One of our nutters lobbed a smoke bomb into the heaving ranks of anoraks only to be jumped by four plainclothes and dragged into the masses stiffoids. I felt it was time to quit, and make my way out of the park, towards the pub and a good night's banter with the troublemakers. All in all, we'd had an amusing day if nothing else.

It wasn't until years later that I met various individuals who'd attended on the 'other side'. Many claimed that our presence, our opposition to them had changed their lives. They'd been seduced by our sheer, iconoclastic, exhilarating behaviour, jealously assuming we'd be off later taking drugs and indulging in weird and wonderful carnality. (In fact I, at least merely got drunk). Meanwhile they'd been ushered onto coaches, singing hymns to enliven the journey back to Dullsville. It's possible their custodians had a point about degenerate subversion after all.

CHAPTER 6

The next couple of years, at least as regards nazis and fascists, were quiet ones. I read up on the subject, and from time to time verbally clashed with the Master Race. Once, upon calling one of the fuckheads an anti-semite, he became rather defensive wailing, "But I love the Arabs!"... I wonder why? I also had plenty of time to ruminate over the peculiarities of the British revolutionary scene, or rather, lack of it. Identical themes churned over in both internal and external discourse.

Unlike the leftists with their ready-made package-deal ideology, I still had no illusions about the working-class, especially when it came to racism of the virulent kind. After all, as I was never tired of reiterating to the increasingly tiresome lefties, what about the tumultuous events of 1968? – a total non-event on our miserable island. The working class I claimed, half seriously, were too busy celebrating England's World Cup victory a couple of years previous to consider building barricades and occupying factories. Why should they have bothered? After all, as I was told with depressing regularity "This is the best fucking country in the world mate..." And to prove it, in that year of 1968, London dockers, meat and fish porters from Smithfield and Billingsgate marched to the House of Commons in their thousands to support Enoch Powell and oppose 'immigration'. My personal experience at work, on the factory floor did little to convince me of the liberal sentiments (let alone revolutionary spirit) of the white working-class. Racism, with older workers at the vanguard, was like a malignant tumour. Those old cunts could make Alf Garnet sound like Leon Trotsky. In a variety of jobs I hardly encountered anything that resembled class consciousness except amongst students. (And that hardly counts does it?) There must have been some explanation of this weird phenomenon. Maybe the peculiar structure of industry in London, small firms, no history of trade-union activity within? Maybe it was a by-product of British imperialism with the indigenous working-class bought off with a comfortable standard of living? Like fuck! I couldn't swallow that one. Wages were pitiful and I couldn't work out how workers with families survived. With all the talk, logic and goodwill in the world, nothing could induce this deeply reactionary mass into accepting black and asian workers into their midst. Not that I had any faith in the classes above, those who benefited most from our misery, ignorance and exploitation. My fervent desire was that us lower orders, us plebs could unite and attack their privileges, their very existence. This was difficult to say the least as our esteemed proletariat were riddled with xenophobia, conservatism, patriotism, deference and sexism of epidemic proportion. There were two great tragedies here. It wasn't the middle and upper classes who were paki-bashing, shoving burning rags through letter boxes, and verbally harassing blacks and asians at work and on the street. And added to this was the grovelling, obsequious attitude shown by the workers to even the lower ranks of the middle class, such as office wallahs and foremen, never mind the more elevated sectors of society. And the final great irony: the middle and upper classes genuinely believed themselves superior whilst the lower orders felt themselves inferior, and believed it too. No wonder I was pissed off, frustrated, ready to explode. But I'd have to wait many years for the biggie.

CHAPTER 7

Around half way through June 1974, Big Sam was quite excited. The National Front were holding a demonstration, culminating with a rally in Conway Hall, Red Lion Square, Holborn. A leftist-liberal outfit, Liberation (formerly the Movement for Colonial Freedom) called for a counter-demonstration, to make its way to the square. Sam thought it looked promising, a chance to have a crack at the Master Race. Of course, the massive police presence had to be taken into consideration. None of our anarchist or even squatter friends showed any enthusiasm. Apparently it was, "Too macho," or, "Had nothing to do with the working-class."

So, it was Sam, myself, and a couple others who made the pilgrimage to Charing Cross Embankment with a single black flag between us. We joined the usual leftist exotica that included a sizeable contingent from the International Marxist Group, bolstered by a large number of students. The most militant (or should that be crazed?) faction were a Maoist grouplet, the Communist Party of England – Marxist-Leninist. We decided to steer clear of all these authoritarians. If we were going to have a crack at the nazis it would have to be under our own steam, allied with non-left elements if at all possible. And nor were we there primarily to fight the police, but then again, if they prevented us from going about our task...

We were ages setting off, roasting under a blazing sun. Sam ventured the opinion, "If we start now, we'll be able to occupy the square; stop the Front holding their rally." I agreed, wilting in the heat. Sam increasingly impatient with proceedings launched into a general attack on jolly old Blighty, its crap politics, boring left, useless anarchists... most of which I couldn't fault. "Did you read the papers?" he moaned, "Someone got crushed to death at a David Cassidy concert. Yet this country hasn't seen a single fatality on a demo, strike or picket for fifty years!" almost spitting this last sentence.

I agreed, but attempted to calm him, "Yeah, it's all a bit lame innit." Sam cooled off, switching to brooding mode. He always meant business, wanted action. And why fucking not?

Eventually the demo moved off, flanked on both side by the usual escort of pigs – something unique to this country, Sam assured me, as was the fact that Britain in those days didn't have a riot police. Wonder why?

The demo seemed fairly militant, shaggy manes in predominance, in keeping with the fashion of the time. Over a thousand strong, we marched rapidly as if to make up for the delay. As we drew close to the square, the tension became electric.

It was obvious some sort of aggro was on the cards. We reached Theobald's Road, the head of the demo turning quickly into North Street, a short narrow road leading directly to the square. Conway Hall was only a few yards away on the left. We didn't see what happened next, but the row was overwhelming. Me and Sam hesitated, unwilling to join the fray, Sam warning me, "We'll be trapped. We've come here for something else."

It didn't take long for people to emerge, dazed from the mêlée, some clutching bloodied heads. We heard the screams and yells of the packed ranks upfront. It was certainly no place to be. A few ineffectual missiles were lobbed at the mounted police who were busy struggling to control their horses in the crush of battle. Truncheons rose, crashing down on the unprotected heads of anti-nazis. Sam turned to me, "Typical. Let's shift further down the road. It's a turkey-shoot in there. Best avoided."

People were now streaming into Theobald's Road, many in considerable distress. Sam grabbed someone he knew, "What's going on? What happened?"

Though clearly dazed, his mate replied, "Those fucking loony Maoists. They steamed straight into the cops. And the pigs lost it. They're pushing us out of the square, truncheoning everyone, sticking the boot in... doing everyone over..." So bringing up the rear of the demo hadn't been such a bad idea after all.

But we didn't allow any of this to put us off as we joined the other demonstrators regrouping on Theobald's Road. By now we could hear the drumbeats of the advancing nazis. And then, their march came into view: a sea of Union Jacks fluttering along Vernon Place leading from New Oxford Street. The flags looked sinister, dangerous too, mounted as they were on pointed steel poles. The nazis halted, drawing up in a line across Southampton Row, facing us in Theobald's Road. Only a few police were in evidence. This had all the hallmarks of a titanic clash, a mass brawl of awesome dimensions. It seemed that everyone was up for it, though at first the typical leftist caution reigned. Neither side moved an inch, the anti-fascists linking arms and chanting, "THE NATIONAL FRONT IS A NAZI FRONT! SMASH THE NATIONAL FRONT!" whilst the Front, accompanied by a steady drumbeat responded with, "THE REDS, THE REDS, WE'VE GOT TO GET RID OF THE REDS!" The NF vanguard 'Leader Guard' was a mean, heavy looking bunch, with short back and sides to a man, and an emphasis on brawn. Certainly none of the usual puny specimens were in evidence up front.

Suddenly a lone figure in a tee shirt burst from the tightly packed ranks of Fronters, halting midway between the two lines. He seemed unhinged, and the sight of our shaggy barnets appeared to tip him into apoplexy. He waved his fists, yelling, "Come on you filthy red scum! I'll 'ave the lot of you!" A small, squat figure emerged from our side, wearing a red beret, his face obscured by a tightly knotted handkerchief. He carried a chunk of wood from a broken banner. No fucking about with formal introductions, he dashed straight up and struck the ranting bonehead directly on the noggin. Wood met wood as blows fell in rapid succession, ending with the self-proclaimed champion scuttling back into the nazi column nursing a re-arranged hairline.

A hearty cheer arose from our side, the entire scene reminiscent of a prelude to a mediaeval battle. But still there was no rush forward from either side. Instead scores of pigs backed up by horses arrived, rushing into the anti-fascists with a force that set everyone reeling. The foot police weren't in a friendly mood and lashed out indiscriminately, grabbing people and giving them a good drubbing before dragging the unfortunate away under arrest, probably to face charges of assault on a police officer.

Me and Sam had remained together throughout. But now the sheer momentum of events separated us. The whole road was total chaos and I found myself isolated, thrust into a group of angry coppers who, faces contorted with rage and crude excitement booted, cuffed and truncheoned everyone unlucky enough to cross their path. One of them grabbed me by the hair, a sharp, almost electric pain surging through my head and down my spine. I had no intention of getting nicked, so I struggled, pulling myself back, steelies glancing against trotters, into the seething, panicked crowd. The pig released his grip, finding himself isolated and in danger. I was now in a flaming temper, liable to do something idiotic and find myself in the back of a meat wagon. But Sam found me. "Fucking pigs," I growled, "tried to nick me, look at this!" pulling generous tufts from my head by way of illustration.

Soon we found ourselves being pushed back into a corner of Red Lion Square with about a hundred other anti-fascists, brawling all the way. Right on the corner itself we ran into a burly police sergeant, separated from his fellow porkers, pulling a frightened woman from behind, his arm around her neck, choking her. "Come on!" shouted Sam, "Let's have the bastard!" In a flash, leaving me trailing, Sam bounded over, landing one full force on the copper's jaw. The big bastard's entire bulk shook and down he went, utterly dazed, disappearing under the feet of the crowd. In went some well aimed boots, my own included. A moment later Sam was back at my side. And what could I do but express my sheer pleasure at his actions.

The cops, however, were gaining control, closing in on us as others shunted the nazis into Red Lion Square. Game over. There was only one thing for us to do. Fuck off, sharp, before we were recognised and picked off. The cops were now in a mean mood, arresting scores, four or five at a time, with plentiful hair-pulling, sly digs and boots.

We left the battleground at speed and catching a tube, made our way across to Notting Hill to a watering hole we occasionally frequented after some of our more hectic encounters. The further away from the action, the better. Sam was fairly nonchalant about his day's work; he'd been in the Israeli army and seen action. He was an active Zionist in spite of being a heavy internationalist anarchist. We never discussed this contradiction. Besides, I wasn't too hot on the Palestinian cause, knowing fuck all about it in those days.

With a few pints swirling around his massive bulk Sam, now grinning, remarked, "That's one pig who'll be in some discomfort for a couple of days. Hope I broke his jaw."

"Yea, you may well have done, Sam. Should have heard the crunch when you made contact. A real one note tune."

A boozy evening followed, surrounded by fellow miscreants and troublemakers. News tricked in, something about there being a fatality. But we were both disappointed that we hadn't managed a full-on with the Master Race.

The next day we met up at Speakers' Corner. Red Lion Square was splashed all over the Sundays. A student, Kevin Gately, had died from a blow to the head during the barney in North Street. Standing well over six foot tall, he'd have presented the ideal target for a mounted cop's truncheon. He'd collapsed, dying on the spot. The Sunday rags were hysterical. The whole episode was the fault of the 'red mob'. You'd have thought a copper had been killed rather than an anti-fascist. A public inquiry followed. The usual crap. The cops were criticised for being a touch heavy-handed, but as usual they were by and large exonerated. The National Front were headline news though, as was the fact that there was violent opposition to the bastards.

CHAPTER 8

It was a long hot summer, though in a meteorological rather than a political sense, with no further occasions for ultra-violence against the Master Race. The Imperial Typewriters dispute was our opportunity. What had happened here was that the predominantly Asian night shift at their Leicester factory had taken industrial action to equalise pay rates and conditions with the mostly white day shift. In a nauseating display of racism and wilful pig-ignorance, the latter pitched in against their fellow workers, taking to the streets behind Union Jacks and banners bearing the slogan 'WHITE WORKERS OF IMPERIAL TYPEWRITERS'. My lefty chums were aghast at how this unionised sector of our glorious, indigenous proletariat could be as xenophobic and racist as the 'backward', 'lumpen' plebs. But despite being at a loss as to how to explain the phenomenon to such enquirers as myself, the left nevertheless, and quite rightly, rallied round in support of the Asian workers.

So it was off to Leicester for me and Sam. There was a National Front demo in support of the white workers of Imperial Typewriters along with the now inevitable counter-demonstration. Both of us were hoping for the opportunity to chin a few nazis. After a dreary ride on a bumpy coach packed full of boring Trots selling papers to one another, we arrived in the dismal town of Leicester. Avoiding the tedious speeches from the platform we headed off to sample the local cuisine, arriving back just as the counter-demo moved off. We joined it, unable to discover where the Front were holding theirs. The anti-fascist organisers were tight-lipped on that one, whilst all the time giving out the impression that we'd confront the enemy sometime later that day. In other words, the usual lefty bullshit: Stalinists and Trots allied with Labour and the unions in the quest for respectability, going all out to avoid aggro. In spite of this the atmosphere on the march was buzzing, many amongst the thousands gathered on the street anticipating some heavy violence against the nazis.

But nothing happened. A large police presence and more importantly, collaboration between the organisers and the filth allied with deliberate misinformation, ensured that we didn't come anywhere near the Master Race. Red Lion Square now seemed like a mere flash in the pan. We cursed, swearing never to go on any more of these marches. We'd get together with those willing, find out the nazis' plans and hammer the fuckers as they assembled. Later, on the journey home, we learned that some demented Maoists had had the same idea and had given the Front's National Activities Organiser a good kicking.

The usual calm and boredom settled on the streets for about a year. But soon, however the whole fascist situation blew up again, propelling myself and others further along the road of political violence.

CHAPTER 9

The National Front's main publicity and successes came in the wake of parliamentary by-elections. Here parties such as the Front came into their own, gaining abnormally large slices of the vote. The Front had become adept at tactics such as saturation canvassing supported by a march through the constituency. Masquerading as part of a legitimate political process, they'd establish or strengthen an already existing branch, picking up fresh members and votes. Aside from some minor interest aroused by the clash in Red Lion Square or the Imperial Typewriters situation, the left hadn't really accepted the disturbing fact that the Front were gaining support in solid working-class areas. And picking up Labour rather than Conservative votes to boot. An unspoken sub-Machiavellian thought of the left was that fascists poached from the Tories, thereby unintentionally giving Labour a helping hand. So but for the efforts of a few enthusiasts the left had been remarkably lax in opposing the racists and nazis. Of course, they didn't want to upset the applecart, bringing political violence onto the streets. This was England, after all.

Within anarchist circles too, I found myself almost alone in urging the necessity of street-level confrontation with fascists and racists. Even the much hinted-at possibility that such aggro might take on a momentum of its own – thereby enlivening the wider social and political arena – was greeted with total indifference. And this, I might add, from even those who claimed to have a class-oriented perspective. I could only surmise that they believed, without a shred of evidence, that the workers' revolution was just around the corner, and that my own crankish obsession with learning to stand upright before entering the marathon was merely an unnecessary diversion on the road to proletarian utopia. My immediate workplace experience, however, was one of a marked turn to the right caused in part by a vicious campaign in the tabloid press, with stories circulating of 'immigrants' being housed in £600-a-week hotels. The social and political atmosphere was poisonous, dripping with unconcealed racism. Attacks on minorities had increased, and despite a thin veneer of tolerance, racism appeared to be fairly acceptable to the vast majority of the white population. And this was racism of a markedly more violent, bitter type: especially when it came to the unskilled, lumpen sector of the white working class. Only a minority – those in mixed relationships perhaps, and some younger workers and militants – were consistently anti-racist. It had become almost like a low-level, undeclared civil war amongst the working class. Black and asian workers were in turn becoming more militant, active in unions such as those in the public service industries.

So my task was proving difficult, compounded by the fact that in anarchist circles at the time class struggle elements were in the minority. The rest were a mish-mash of middle class, self-styled 'anti-sexist' men, bourgeois feminists, pacifists, lifestylists, revolutionary anoraks, and devotees of the latest political, mystical and fashionable trend. Their pathetic excuses for not offering support ranged from the predictable to the unbelievable. Maybe they didn't fancy getting their mitts dirty, or was it that they were scared to disturb the illusion of 'socialism in one room'? I sometimes thought to myself that maybe they had a fear of the lower orders, myself included. All well and good, but it infuriated me to the core when things became whispered and personal. Those of us who wanted a crack were designated 'macho', 'sexist' or both. And this came from thick and fast from all sides, compounded with the foul hypocrisy that accompanies such middle-class posturings. After all, it was disturbingly common for geezers to combine a taste for spouting this garbage in public with a penchant for a bit of non-consensual violence back home with the missus (sorry, partner). Or for those on the receiving end, it was easy enough, by way of a weird form of projection, to take it out on such 'sexist', 'macho' scapegoats as myself and my accomplices.

What wound me up most, however, were the bearded pacifists and their floppy chicks who continually prattled on about how, "The racists and fascists are human beings too." Along with the inevitable, "Because you believe in violence, you're just as bad as they are." Apart from such sentiments being screeched in a most infuriating tone, the inference here naturally was that since I should know better I was probably worse. And what with being a 'sexist' too...

Others would bleat, with the usual self-righteous conviction, "Why don't you just try talking to them?" And occasionally I did rise to the bait. "But I do... admittedly it's usually more a dialogue of fist and boot... but don't worry, we'll get down to the philosophical stuff sooner or later." Calculated to wind them up, such lines would normally produce incredulity. My 'unlibertarian' posturing was an anathema to them. But for me, it was a case of, "Bollocks to that." I knew what I wanted, where the future lay, and it certainly didn't involve acting like some creeping Jesus.

By 1975 I'd noticed an increasing amount of fascist graffiti, posters and stickers appearing on the streets. Having a job that involved working outdoors, clearing away rubbish in the streets, it was difficult to avoid. First of all there were the National Front stickers and posters. The most ridiculous offering, but obviously striking a chord somewhere amongst the brain-damaged sectors was of a wizened old woman staring out of a window, the caption reading 'IF ONLY I WAS BLACK'. Their logic was unfathomable, but then racism and fascism were never exactly logical. Rumour had it that razor blades were secreted beneath these stickers, but I never came across any as I ripped them off by the hundred. Nastier, more insidious were the uncredited stickers such as the one featuring a cartoon trio of sinister, leering Sikhs reading, 'WE WANT YOUR JOBS, WE WANT YOUR HOMES, WE WANT YOUR COUNTRY'. Obviously the handsome, virile übers who'd designed that one had no fears for their women. Another masterpiece of propaganda had a heavy-looking gorilla face with the words 'INDEPENDENCE FOR BRIXTON'. Frankly the gorilla looked more like a typical National Front goon than anything else. It should have read 'JOIN THE NATIONAL GRUNT'.

One amusing interlude intervened before I was sucked into a vortex of extreme political violence. Although I'd long since stopped my regular visits to Speakers' Corner, I found myself at a loose end one grim winter's afternoon, so dug out a warm coat and headed out. I stood around for a while with a couple of Park nutters taking the piss out of the glazed-eyed followers of some portly guru who'd proclaimed himself divine. Some idiots, no matter how well educated, will believe anything. My attention, however, was drawn to a large Union Jack. Could it be the National Front? If so, things would warm up for sure.

This outfit turned out to be a collection of hardcore no nonsense nazis with the ponderous title 'The National Democratic Freedom Movement'. I'd never heard of them, but this outfit of Aryan beauties had travelled all the way from Leeds to educate us dumb Londoners in the finer ways of National Socialism. The dozen or so numbskulls had arranged themselves around a portable platform. None of the usual trainspotter gear for this lot, they were mostly young lads, dressed in leather, seemingly picked for their impeccable blond looks; beautiful and repulsive simultaneously. No point arguing with this bunch, I strode off to find reinforcements. Soon enough, I'd located some heavy Zionists, some of whom I'd been matey with for years. Although I disapproved of their politics and they of mine, we were all up for a round of nazi-bashing. And these Zionists were big, heavy bastards. So about half a dozen of us pushed our way through the crowd of spectators as their old-fashioned demagogue worked himself up into a right old frenzy. He spewed out the usual garbage about Jewish control, coloured immigration, communism and the rest, and although I'd heard the same stuff many times before, it still made me feel angry. We listened with remarkable patience to this swill, all things considered. Then came exchanged insults, threats. The nazis clustered around their speaker, ready to repulse an attack, which certainly looked imminent. The majority of the bemused audience were tourists who didn't have a clue what was going down. With great restraint, we allowed the meeting to continue until their Fuhrer, sporting a toothbrush moustache, mounted the rostrum. He launched into a passable imitation of the fella from the beer cellar, but we'd had enough, laughing our attack, flinging the bastard from his perch. Fists flew, übers scattered, their Fuhrer crumpled into a heap after his tumble, his platform reduced to matchwood over him as he struggled to his feet. Only a couple of Nordic warriors stood their ground, but jaw-crunching blows from the Zionists and slamming kicks from me and the nutters put an end to the contest. The police arrived, too late for their purposes. The nazis had fled. And we ambled off after a warning, tourists dumbfounded, unable to utter a word. Well warmed, we strode off to the nearest café for a coffee, happy with our afternoon's unexpected fun. We never heard from that particular outfit again.

CHAPTER 10

The National Front announced a 'MARCH AGAINST MUGGERS' to be held on September 6th 1975. By remarkable coincidence, this was also a Jewish holiday. Given the violent criminal behaviour of their rank and file – not to say their leaders – the 'yid' and 'queer' rollers, paki bashers galore, there was more than a touch of sick irony involved. This march was just another feeble excuse to flaunt their racist credentials; the muggers in question fitting the pathetic stereotype of young black lads. To drive the point home the nazis would march behind a banner reading, '80% OF MUGGERS ARE BLACK – 85% OF VICTIMS ARE WHITE'. Their route would take them from Bethnal Green to Hoxton, the latter a white working class racist stronghold. Hoxton then was a drab miserable shit-hole of crumbling council blocks and more recently erected concrete monstrosities, where blacks and asians walked the streets in trepidation. No one, least of all the Front themselves, really believed that the cracked pavements and dimly lit alleyways of that particular stretch of town were infested with footpads originating from sunnier climes. But that wasn't going to prevent the Master Race from masquerading as victims.

The left had organised a counter-demonstration assembling near the Front starting point. Circulating amongst the lefties and anti-racists it became clear to me that here would be no deliberate confrontation, not even an attempt to peacefully block the fascists by sheer force of superior numbers. But this is just what I'd come to expect from demonstrations dominated by Labour, the Communist Party and trade unions, with the usual sprinkling of Trotskyite grouplets flogging pathetic rags to the already converted.

It didn't take too long to locate a few dissatisfied souls who were more than willing to have a crack verbally or physically should opportunity present itself. A few thousand anti-fascists had gathered to oppose the Front, but a large number of police were on duty to prevent any fun and games. The atmosphere surrounding the counter-demo was tranquil, passive even though they'd mustered a respectable three to four thousand. Knots of local white youngsters hung around, looking as though they'd commit to the Front column. But I'd already figured that a barney wasn't on the cards apart from on the margin of events. Too many cops. Not enough people willing to steam in. So it was a case of the same old boring hanging around, cooling heels. I was entertained by some old Jewish women. They clued me up about 'the old days', opposing Mosley and his blackshirt scum. True devotees of the well-lobbed half-brick were these old ducks, one of whom described how they'd roll out hundreds of marbles into the road under the hooves of police horses, thereby causing the animals to slip, shedding their porcine load. Couldn't help wondering why we didn't repeat that ideal scenario.

Frantic pig activity indicated that the Front were ready to move off. Their Orange-Order style drum corps struck up with a chilling sound. Boy Scouts they weren't, Hitler Youth more like. Large concentrations of filth prevented us from rushing the nazi phalanx as it goose-stepped off. We were determined to have some form of confrontation. Meanwhile the counter-demo moved off in the opposite direction, "THE NATIONAL FRONT IS A NAZI FRONT, SMASH THE NATIONAL FRONT!" they chanted, as usual. We wouldn't be seeing many of them for the rest of the day.

Drizzle began to fall, an autumnal chill in the air. But meteorological considerations were the last thing on our minds. Between a hundred and a hundred and fifty of us ducked through side streets leaving the plod standing in the road getting wet. Eventually after much expenditure of breath, losing a handful of people on the way, we drew up parallel to the Front march, verbally harassing them from the pavement. The nazis were well guarded by the police who walked in ranks alongside their parade. Even without the pigs it would have been suicidal to have launched an attack. I noticed that some of the kids and youth who'd been lurking previously at Bethnal Green had joined us, warming to our verbal abuse of the Fronters. As the nazis marched along, ducking the occasional beer can, those of us with the loudest voices raised the tempo, pouring out insults, mostly personal stuff rather than boring political slogans, although we did manage a few hearty 'SEIG HEIL's complete with accompanying stiff arm gestures. Bet they'd have loved to have returned the compliment, but it was the Union Jack and not the Swastika that they were flying today. The fascists were on best behaviour in fact, stewards pleading with the marchers to ignore us. Some however, couldn't resist the deep-seated temptation, making anti-semitic motions with their paws, rubbing their noses, pretending to flick banknotes between thumb and forefinger. The marchers were predominately middle-aged, male, shambolically attired though doubtless considering themselves 'smart'. Many on the march, including small gangs of youth, seemed somewhat disappointed by the lack of opportunity to engage in fisticuffs with the dirty red degenerates and hippy perverts who dogged them through the empty streets.

Me and a bunch of young trouble-makers, along with some local youth, managed to get to the head of the march relatively unhampered by the police. They were too busy keeping the factions apart. This worked to our advantage because the Front were now surrounded by the police, reduced to strutting impotently in their ill-fitting jackboots, unable even to hand out their leaflets. And nor could sympathisers join their march. The head of the column contained the leadership and a set of gentlemen from the labouring fraternity, selected for their capacious bulks rather than their great intellects. The main banner displayed the 'muggers' slogan, but appeared to have been partly censored on the orders of the police. It depicted a silhouette of an old lady with handbag, glasses flying off, coshed by another silhouette whose features had been blanked out with the word 'CENSORED'. It took no great flight of imagination to picture what had been hidden from view. We rained abuse on the leadership, a seedy looking crowd of hate-merchants. Most of it was extremely personal, such as remarks about various sexual peccadilloes of certain characters that would do little to increase the numbers of the Aryan race. The local kids were now enjoying themselves, getting into the spirit and regaling the Front with cries of "WANKERS!" "TOSSERS!" Hoxton, however, appeared strangely deserted. We seemed to be the only people on the streets. The mobs of frenzied racists that I'd half expected, but forgotten about in the heat of the moment had thankfully failed to materialise. Even within the march itself, most of the banners were from branches well outside the area, and the marchers appeared confused by the lack of local support. The kids by now were leading the chants of disapproval and some gained the road in front of the march. The streets narrowed and police now swooped, pushing the kids off the road, wielding batons, hemming us all against railings too high to be scaled. Kicks and blows were exchanged with the uniforms. The nazis were funnelled though the resulting bottleneck and we suffered a handful of arrests. Both sides were relatively content at the afternoon's work as the Front eventually made their way to a rally in Hoxton Square.

Around two hundred of us were left milling around, including the kids, who were up for more action. We roamed fruitlessly, exchanging pleasantries with the few locals who'd ventured out. The kids it seemed, had turned against the Front because they appeared to be collaborating with the police. Few, if any, kids in that neck of the urban jungle harbour pleasant sentiments as regards the Old Bill. They don't call 'em cuntstables for nothing. Had the tables been turned, I'm sure the kids would have joined in on the Front's side. We were more fun, that's all. So we wandered around Hoxton for a while, unmolested, then drifted off to a green space to meet up with those we'd lost on the way. Unlike the nazis we'd picked up support en route. Although alert, somewhat pumped up with adrenaline, my guard had dropped. A bottle thrown from a high-rise disintegrated into powder at my feet. Another couple of inches and I'd have been a goner. Relatively unperturbed, I caught up with the others. Some diehards wanted to go over to Old Street tube where the fascists were sure to be heading after their rally. Saner voices prevailed. We'd be outnumbered, the Old Bill's patience would have been long spent. Didn't fancy a kicking on the streets, another in the meatwagon and a night in the cells. Some of the more hostile local youth were busy arguing with leftists who'd started to drift in now the action was finished. We decided to quit whilst ahead, relatively satisfied with the day's events.

Leaving Hoxton I came across one of my more vociferous critics: one of the self-styled 'non-violent', 'non-sexist' anarchists. He too was surrounded by angry youth. "You've never done a day's work in your life, cunt!" they spat, "Come on, apart from being on the fucking dole, what do you do for a living?"

"I'm a musician," Mister Non-Violent simpered back.

"A musician?" rejoined his tormentors, "They're all fucking queers!"

Given the locale, these lads were in a fairly restrained mood. Maybe a nearby vanload of pigs tempered their spirits. In other circumstances it might have been down to me to step in and assist my fellow 'anarchist'. But no, a 'sexist', 'macho' was I? Perhaps a kicking from some more 'unreconstructed' proles might have been something of an eye opener for this particular creep.

CHAPTER 11

Sunny Hoxton was also the scene of a notable incident the following year. A pleasant spring morning in 1976 saw around four hundred nervous lefties, trade unionists, and various representatives of local ethnic groups gather on the edge of Ridley Road Market in Dalston. The occasion was an anti-racist march deep into the heart of Hoxton, where there'd recently been an escalating series of racist attacks. I'd certainly kept away from the place since the 'March Against Muggers', having few occasions to visit that particular lumpen Cockney stronghold, but given the humiliation the Front had suffered on that occasion, I was confident that today would be a pleasant stroll. If our luck was in, we might even run into a few isolated nazis and give them a good kicking; and thence retire to a pleasant Portobello watering hole for an evening's fun. Such was my naivety. What I'd neglected to take into account was the fact that most of the local support we'd received the previous September was due mainly to the Front's perceived collaboration with the Old Bill: the fact that they'd crassly marched into Hoxton under heavy police protection. They'd marked themselves out as strangers – and in Hoxton they didn't like strangers. Nor anyone, really.

Although I'd arrived alone from another part of town, I'd arranged to meet up with a resident of Hoxton, a cynical but realistic geezer called Rosie. Despite being Jewish and blessed with the name Rosen, he'd somehow managed to survive in that racist menagerie. Maybe the locals were too busy abusing, harassing and attacking those of a darker hue to worry about someone inconspicuous . As I stood about waiting for the off, I met a few lefties I knew and was on good terms with. I noticed that for this march, they'd ditched their paper selling and were in mufti. What literature there was being pedalled came from the Communist Party and their tiny front groups. Most of them seemed to be elderly veterans who wouldn't be up to a full-scale punch up with any opposition. Still there were plenty of fresh-faced hacks from the Young Socialists (most of whom still looked older than me) and Militant. I had one of these jokers tell me that most anarchists eventually went on to become fascists. I gently reminded him that Mosley had been high ranking in his own shitty Labour Party. It passed the time.

Rosie finally showed, hot foot from Hoxton market, flushed: "You'd better warn your mates, anyone you know, there's loads of Front down there. They've been gathering all morning and they're in an ugly mood." The numbers for the demonstration had swelled to about six hundred, but I was losing confidence fast. And Rosie was no alarmist. We certainly couldn't rely on the police to provide adequate protection, which was something that I found demeaning anyway, whatever the circumstances. But as Rosie and the Trots were determined to go ahead, I joined them, bringing up the rear. Rosie pulled up his collar, plonking on a bobble hat as a hasty disguise, "Better off safe than sorry, Mart," and so we shuffled off along Kingsland Road exchanging horror stories about Hoxton. It was a mild, pleasant morning, with no indication of the storms that lay ahead.

The march filed along through Kingsland Waste, turning right into the appropriately named Nuttal Street leading us to the bottom of Hoxton Market. An air of trepidation settled over our assembled ranks.

The locals were waiting. Nutters indeed. And they weren't exactly overjoyed to see us. A guttural roar of disapproval emerged by way of greeting. This crowd of crazed individuals was mainly ordinary Saturday shoppers rather than hardcore Front. Frenzied old bids brandished packets of Daz: 'Washes Whiter than White!' Horrendous curses emanated from snaggle-toothed hags and red-faced Cockney geezers in cloth caps and braces, "GET BACK TO RUSSIA YOU FUCKIN' COMMIE BASTARDS!", "RED SCUM!", "HAVE A BARF!" Only the sizeable police presence prevented a large-scale punch up. The march, collectively reeling from all this naked hostility veered to the right, away from the baying mob. We weren't out of the woods yet, though. A somewhat flustered mate of Rosie's joined us, "Watch yourselves! There's loads of Front further up. It looks like Planet of the Apes up there." And though there were no vines hanging from the lampposts to enable the simian Master Race to swing to their rendezvous, we began to fear that the real jungle did indeed lie ahead.

Knots of stunted locals continued to abuse us as the march progressed: "PAKI LOVERS!" "NIGGER LOVERS!" "GIT YER FUCKIN' 'AIR CUT!" Coming to Hoxton had been a big mistake. But there was no time to ponder. As we approached the roundabout, our route back to Kingsland Road and safety, a couple of hundred of the finest specimens the Aryan race has produced awaited, clutching Union Jacks and placards. On the side of dismal council block, large whitewashed letters proclaimed, 'SUPPORT THE WHITE RHODESIANS'. How appropriate, how relevant to the inhabitants of this run down, economically deprived locale: and in the midst of such grimness they could still be internationalist!

The assembled apes were of the larger varieties of the species. Many were lacking skin on their knuckles, a result of numerous brawls perhaps, or was it from dragging them along the pavements as they meandered from the bookies to the pub? There was no time for further zoological investigations, however, as the sky blackened, and not with storm clouds but with a torrential shower of missiles – a veritable Agincourt no less. Rotten fruit (though no bananas, as the apes had probably scoffed them all), bottles, lumps of wood, smoke bombs, all flew our way. The head of the march, taking the full brunt of this assault, momentarily shuddered to a halt. Making no attempt to disperse or arrest the perpetrators, even the most blatant individuals, the Old Bill did manage to prevent some of the more deranged nazis from physically hurling themselves into the ranks of demonstrators. It stuck me that quite a few of these beer-bellied, cloth-capped, multi-scarred racists were middle-aged and almost certainly part of the indigenous population. Hoxton, what a fucking place! Fortunately however, their initially liberal expenditure of munitions meant that little was available for the tail of the march. So apart from the odd stray missile here and there, all we had to endure was a sea of horrible, contorted faces spitting hate, grolly and venom. After what felt like an eternity, but was in reality a few minutes we left the nazi mob behind, who sent us on our way with a rousing chorus of 'Rule Britannia'.

A collective sigh of relief passed through our battered ranks only to be temporarily interrupted further up the road. Here, a cluster of Union Jack waving youths from a Front breakaway group, the National Party, awaited. We were subjected to the usual patriotic grunts, although nothing heavy took place as we passed them by. Eventually, outside a cinema in Kingsland Road, the march halted. A couple of understandably shaken speakers form the local Trades' Council attempted, without success, to kindle enthusiasm. Rosie noticed some nazis filtering up the side streets. A few hovered on the fringes. A speaker from 'Liberation' was announced. I heard some of the nazis mutter, "Must be a queer." Time, I felt to leave for the sanctuary of Dalston. Rosie was amused to see members of the local Communist Party, mostly elderly folk, ducking into the cinema. "Bit old for Saturday morning pictures aren't they?" We wandered off for a drink and chat about the Hoxton love-in. The main thrust of the discussion was one simple theme: NEVER AGAIN! Next time we'd reverse the roles, give the Front a taste of their own medicine. I was well up for that. Payback. With interest.

CHAPTER 12

April 1976, I noticed an enigmatic sticker appearing around London, advertising a 'Patriots' March' from East Smithfield to Trafalgar Square. This was to be held on April 24th, on the same Saturday the National Front would be staging a provocative march through a black and asian area in Bradford. From the look of the 'Patriots March' sticker, it didn't take a Sherlock Holmes to figure out that the fully fledged, unabashed nazi group the British Movement were behind it. It was no coincidence that BM stickers everywhere accompanied the 'Patriot' ones. It wouldn't be far from the truth to say that the BM regarded the Front as 'Kosher Fascists' or even 'Reds'.

Being skint at the time, an away day in Bradford was out of the question, but a stroll down to the Square was within budgetary limits, so come the appointed day, I turned up with a couple of aficionados. We found only anti-nazis in attendance, with plenty of familiar faces. There was no question of treating the BM to a mere barracking: these nazis were totally hardcore. Even a kicking wouldn't be therapeutic, there was just no knocking sense into this stiff-armed crew. So a couple of hundred of us stood around awaiting the nazis. Fearing the onset of rigor mortis, we began to drift off up the Strand into Fleet Street, hoping to meet them head on. And sure enough, there they were, protected by the usual massive phalanx of cops, a few hundred shaven-headed nazis. They were all similarly attired: black leather zip-ups, white shirts, black ties and Doc Martens. Some of these creatures sported armbands with the BM sun wheel insignia. A political uniform – highly illegal. The police, however, were more interested in the opposition, with a large detachment from the Special Patrol Group containing us on the pavement. Both sides were easily outnumbered by cops, so chances of a barney seemed remote. Despite the best efforts of the SPG we managed to keep abreast of the Hitler Youth clones and boneheads, exchanging insults. No point Seig Heiling this vile bunch as they would likely take it for a compliment. Only as the nazis entered the Square did an opportunity present itself for a belated crack. The police formation did a quick Busby Berkeley choreographic job, creating a gap that allowed us to steam in from the other side of the previously erected barriers. Fist and boot flew for a few brief moments, contact made, but the cops were on top of the situation within seconds. By sheer numbers they separated us, driving the anti-nazis to a remote corner of the square. This manoeuvre effectively cleared the remainder of the square, however, leaving the BM speakers free to harangue flocks of assembled pigeons. I'd managed to land a couple of good boots with my steelies: my sole contribution to the aggro.

Next day I read in the Sundays about the near riot in Bradford. Police were attacked as they tried to escort the Front though Lumb Lane, and police vehicles were overturned. Human barricades linked arms across the road, preventing the Front from taking their intended route. I recognised some anarchos with black flags up in the front of the photographs. Maybe I should have made a better effort to have stumped up the fare for a day return. I certainly felt I'd missed out on a good day's entertainment.

CHAPTER 13

The National Front persisted with their tactic of standing candidates in parliamentary by-elections, gaining fairly respectable votes, sometimes measured in the low thousands. This provided the nazis with an opportunity to gain publicity and recruits, reaping their bitter harvest mainly in working-class areas. Here disillusionment with the Labour government was running high, and of course these areas contained plenty of indigenous working-class racist morons who needed little encouragement to register a protest vote to the fascists. And more besides. Racist attacks were on a steady increase. Such an occasion was the East Thurrock by-election in Essex. The Front announced that they would be marching in support of their candidate through a town called Grays near Tilbury Docks. Vaguely knowing the area, with the dump lying within easy reach of London, I fancied a trip out, a Saturday afternoon dust-up. Especially since the übers were due to parade their latest trophy, the nazi hunger striker Robert Relf, recently released from prison after breaching the race-relations act by advertising his house for sale to 'whites only'.

Try as I did, I found it difficult to persuade anybody in the anarchist scene to accompany me on this jaunt. Only one intrepid soul, Jeb, motivated by sheer curiosity, made the journey from Fenchurch Street station. This part of Essex was a right craphole, an estimated one-tenth of the constituency being gravel pits and rubbish dumps. Arriving at the windswept station after a journey on a dirty, creaking train me and Jeb felt like Butch Cassidy and the Sundance Kid as they alighted from the train in rural Bolivia. Only the lamas were absent. We considered jumping back on the train for the return journey as the streets appeared deserted. Grays is a small town though and I had some sort of an idea where the Front would be assembling. So, curiosity getting the better of us, we headed off in that direction. Eventually we met up with a couple of dozen of anti-fascists. They'd already been involved in an altercation with the Front's typically unsavoury candidate, a well-known wife-beater, chinned him and fucked off to regroup. We got as near as we could to the Front's starting point until the numbers of police in the area made it impossible to continue any further. Maybe it was for the best. There seemed to be a fair number of the bastards, hundreds of Front, many more heading their way. We were heavily outnumbered and there was much hurried debate as to what thirty of us could do against five hundred and growing. The odds didn't look good. The police, though I was loath to admit it, would provide us with some protection that day.

The head of the Front march assembled with the usual forest of Union Jacks and drum corps. Propped up between a couple of muscular primates was the cadaverous figure of Relf, the star turn. I couldn't restrain myself, yelling, "And the first to go will be the old and the weak!" There wasn't much point in competing with all the noise, however, so we let the head of the march pass by before turning our attention to the rank and file. I was quite alarmed as it became obvious that their ranks contained many locals, family groups and youngsters. It was a boiling hot day, unusual as the Front tended to bring grey skies. Having reviewed the situation, I led the cat-calling. Sometimes sophisticated, mainly crude and vulgar. Glancing at a banner reading 'NATIONAL FRONT TRADE UNIONISTS' one word was sufficient, chanted continuously, "SCABS! SCABS! SCABS!" They didn't like the truth. The family groups contained, even for Essex, an abnormally large number of peroxides, most of whom were fairly free with the counter-abuse: "FUCKIN' COMMIE SCUM!", "PAKI LOVERS!" A group of teenage girls passed by wearing tee-shirts advertising "DAVE'S DISCO", not that I frequented such establishments, but I certainly wouldn't be getting on down at Dave's. If I did, I'd never get up again.

As we warmed to the task, a few of us became quite bold, menacing individual marchers, piling on the sarcasm, the insults, not really bothering with the traditional boring anti-nazi slogans. Some responded personally: "You long 'aired cunt! You're just a fuckin' wanker!"

To which I chipped back, "At least I can manage that. Unlike you, parading your sexual impotence through the fuckin' streets." Our superior repartee reduced most of the numbheads to a surly silence.

As we wound round the back streets of the appropriately named Grays, the police did little to restrain us. We were few and they'd concentrated their resources at the head of the march. We became more daring, throwing caution to the wind, lobbing the odd can, offering them out, "Come on then, we'll 'ave the lot of you! We ain't scared of you mangy tossers, you're only good for throwing kids into gas chambers!" Sooner or later something had to give. And it did. They broke ranks, charging through the police, attacking us with placards. No time for repose, reflection or retreat. Me, Jeb and about a dozen of us stood our ground until we were pushed into front garden walls. The Old Firm of Fist and Boot swung into action as placards smashed down on heads. Adrenaline ran high as we fought back, my steel capped size tens ploughing into the knees of one outstandingly hideous specimen of Essex manhood. Before we were overwhelmed, police reinforcements waded in. As the Fronters were tooled up, the cops were rough, even arresting a few, dragging them off unceremoniously, their bottle-blonde spouses screeching, "Leave 'im alone! Why don't you nick them fuckin' communist perverts?" Never mind the thickos who'd just steamed in, I was more wary of the female of the subspecies. The cops made no attempt to disperse us, however, so nursing minor wounds we carried on with the harassment, even when me and Jeb had been separated from the others.

Eventually, we arrived at the school where they were to hold their Nuremberg rally re-enactment. The afternoon's aggro had me at full verbal throttle, and I poured vitriol on the marchers as they were herded into the building. "Pathetic!" "Call yourselves the Master Race?" "Look at the state of 'im! More a sack of potatoes than a human being!"

One individual shouted back, "You should be with us!"

This had me temporarily stumped. But I was soon roaring back, "Do me a favour! If I wanted to mix with the likes of you and your mates, I'd go down to the monkeyhouse at the zoo!" It always felt good to reverse their twisted racist logic, to confront their arrogance with their miserable reality.

By now the police had singled me out, an inspector warning me in classic fashion, "Right chummy, you've had your fun, now bugger off or I'll nick you and your mate." Mission accomplished, we returned to the station, spending the return journey in animated conversation. Jeb had never seen anything like that before, and never cared to do so again. Still, he agreed it had been a worthwhile excursion. We'd made up in verbal clout for what we'd lacked in numbers.

That afternoon's events were a microcosm of the dangers facing us during those times. Plenty of working class people were going for the racist crap. You couldn't discount the painful evidence of your own eyes, your own experience. I wanted to ratchet things up, bring out ever more folk to oppose the fascists head to head, before we were swamped by this growing racist tide. The Front polled over three thousand votes in the East Thurrock by-election.

CHAPTER 14

There had been disturbances on the streets of Southall the previous weekend. A young asian lad had been stabbed to death in what was widely held to have been a racial attack. The next day, spontaneous protests broke out in the streets of that west London town. During minor clashes, cars were stoned. The summer of '76 had really hotted up, the tabloid press fanning the flames with customary relish. Hardly a day went by at my workplace without an argument breaking out about 'immigrants' or 'immigration'. No need to elaborate. By now I'd endured it a thousand and one times. On the Saturday following the Southall disturbances, a march against – surprise, surprise – 'immigration' was announced, taking place in West Ham. This area was a stronghold of Alf Garnettism, racist attacks and general working-class density. And I'm not talking about overcrowded dwellings. This march was organised by the National Party, a 'populist' split from the National Front, led by a George Wallace lookalike, John 'Kinky' Read. Ideology had little to do with this split. Rather, it was a case of personality differences. So this new outfit was just another nazi crew parading with the Union Jack, peddling the same old fascist crap. In the poisonous atmosphere of that summer, the vile racist message was gaining rapid credence among elements of the proles. And from my vantage point, in particular when it came to the workplace, it appeared that the majority held such views.

I decided to attend the counter-demo as I wasn't all that familiar with the West Ham area. I was intending to meet up with some fellow enthusiasts, split off from the march, find the National Party morons and patiently explain to them the benefits of a multi-cultural society and proletarian solidarity.

Prior to this excursion, I met up with a couple of folk down Whitechapel High Street. That morning there was to be a demo against police harassment and racist violence, a semi-spontaneous event organised by the local Bengalis. So a few of us joined them at the meeting point outside the Naz cinema in Brick Lane, destination, the nearby Leman Street police station. Personally, I was only too willing to join in, having had aggro myself from the bastards on the streets of Whitechapel and Aldgate. "Searching for drugs." "Reason to believe you may be carrying a concealed weapon." It wasn't just Bengalis that got grief from the filth, but it seemed that they were only ones willing to do anything about it. The indigenous white population mostly supported the cops' hassling of people with dark skin, hippies, squatters... many keen themselves to provide assistance in this department, all too frequently working freelance, lobbing bricks through windows, administering kickings in side streets. Only a handful of whites were on the demo, all of us planning to shoot down to West Ham later.

The march itself was extremely militant: a huge crowd of pissed-off asians numbering well over a thousand. No banners or placards, just a surge of anger and bodies towards the local cop-shop. People working in the sweatshops were forcibly dragged out onto the street, literally press-ganged into joining the march. It had all the appearances of an unofficial one day strike, but being from outside the community we didn't totally grasp the dynamic of what was going down. We kept company with a gang of young asian Cockneys who were also travelling to West Ham later. It was only a short stroll to the police station, but the journey wasn't without incident. A pub door swung open to reveal beer-bellied loudmouths shouting the usual garbage, "FUCK OFF BACK TO YOUR OWN COUNTRY!" Plus the old standby from the fifties, "YOU'RE ALL ON NATIONAL ASSISTANCE!" A brief hail of bottles and stones soon saw these creatures retreating back into their drinking den.

The otherwise deserted streets echoed with the chants of the crowd as it neared the police station. It was a scorching hot day, some dark clouds hanging overhead only adding to the electric brooding atmosphere. We were looking forwards to an interesting day. The police simply bolted the doors, cowering inside, as the odd missile cracked against the façade. They didn't venture outside, sensibly. The mob remained in position, awaiting speeches from community leaders. Time, however, was pressing. We had a bus to catch.

Our journey through the East End took us through an area with which I was well familiar, until that is we came to the great divide: Bow Creek, the gateway to Canning Town. Despite being a hardcore Londoner, I'd rarely set foot in this decaying, semi-derelict rundown part of town. This place had a reputation as a geographically larger version of Hoxton, hostile territory. We piled off the bus that had been virtually full ever since we'd left Aldgate. The anti-fascist march was starting in Canning Town, near a flyover. The usual rag, tag and bobtail of leftist exotica were gathered, along with many local Asians plus the increasing number of non-aligned who just wanted to have a crack at the nazis. Surprisingly, perhaps a sign of the troubled times, there was a larger than expected turn out of anarchists and assorted troublemakers, around a hundred in all. I'd already decided to join them, but first I treated myself to a perambulation, an opportunity to meet the natives. Sure enough, a group of them were arguing ferociously with some hapless members of the Socialist Workers' Party. Same old crap, a dialogue of deaf and daft. This time, however, my ears pricked up, hearing a story that I'd endured in various permutations at least four different times that very month. "My niece married one of 'em. And you know what?" spouted some peroxide with dark roots, "She weren't allowed outdoors. An' when she was, she 'ad to wear one of them 'eadscarf things, walk behind 'im. A virtual prisoner she was." The lefties didn't know how to respond, trotting out stuff like, "Blame the bosses, not the blacks," only to be met with a, "Yeah, but the bosses didn't rape my sister." The leftists might well have been saying, "Blame the anthropomorphism of Capital, not the blacks."

But I didn't deal in such abstractions, so I waded straight in, pushing the gormless lefties aside: "I've heard this same fairytale all over town! As if your sister or niece or whatever would marry a fuckin' paki as you call 'em... fuckin' leave it out willya." Result, instant violence. She lunged at me full force. I neatly sidestepped, leaving her bulk to tumble into the lefties. I departed pronto with a barrage of colourful east London expletives ringing in my ears. The lefties weren't too pleased. Obviously they'd been winning the argument, and I'd cost them a potential recruit. As if.

I rejoined the anarcho section, though apart from a couple of black flags, they didn't stand out in the crowd now numbering many thousands. Off it set, in a determined mood under a blazing sun. Within a couple of hundred yards, a salvo of heavy beer glasses and bottles flew into the march from outside a nearby pub. There followed a surreal moment as the assailants struck up a chorus of the West Ham anthem, "I'M FOREVER BLOWING BUBBLES..." The demonstrators replied with their own ammunition, which soon had the opposition retreating into the shelter of the pub. I'd noticed the relatively small numbers of police in attendance. Maybe they were overstretched, guarding the National Party march in East Ham, our final destination.

We were now heading straight for East Ham. No need to split off, to look for the nazis and racists. They'd probably come looking for us anyhow. And it would be their mistake today, for we were angry, tooled up with lumps of timber, bottles, half-bricks tucked snugly into our jackets. We didn't have to wait long. Every inch of our progress was contested with shouts, curses, bottles and stones hurled by enraged cretins. Their modest numbers meant the cops were virtually powerless to prevent attacks and retaliation. Some rednecks stood on the flat roofs of shops and balconies, chucking debris, screaming racist abuse. We returned fire, forcing them to retreat. Many friendly locals, however, joined the march. We swelled in numbers and confidence, some of us brazenly displaying our hardware, offering out any hostile thickos. Our attackers weren't for the most part hardened nazis. It didn't take a political genius to figure our their voting sympathies: Labour or Front. This, after all was a working class heartland, where a simple, unsophisticated attitude to life ruled. In other words, a place abundant with racist morons. Eventually, some time in the not too distant future, we'd find ourselves in deep shit unless we neutralised or won these people over. But how? The only dialogue taking place here was the old fashioned Saturday afternoon shindig, consisting of half bricks and lumps of four-by-two. I suppose it was a start, open confrontation, let's have it out, the language they understood. Get them thinking in the aftermath, nursing a sore head. Such was my understanding. The majority of anarcho-drones disagreed, seeing no alternative to their usual bland moralising. Upbraided, all I could do was retort, "This is the fuckin' east end, not Hampstead!"

But there was little time for metaphysical speculations today. The sky clouded over as the march became more compact, with young asians and a significant number of whites spoiling for a direct confrontation with the nazis. Tension mounted as we passed from West to East Ham, even though the attacks were growing less frequent. More police appeared. Drops of rain began to fall, adding to the crackling static feeling that set your hair on end. We sensed that we were near to the fascists. More hostile crowds had gathered, some being restrained by the cops. Not that they'd have dared to launch an all out assault owing to our numerical superiority and obvious determination. I thought I heard a shot ring out, but there was no panic. Maybe it was just a firework explosion. But if the opposition had started to blaze away with shooters, it wouldn't have surprised me. Such was the atmosphere.

Most of the thugs now harassing us had clearly been on the National Party march. Some of the younger idiots were covered in racist stickers, some even sporting the aforementioned 'INDEPENDENCE FOR BRIXTON!' masterpiece; irony indeed given the simian features of these unfortunate specimens.

As we arrived at Plashet Park, our destination for the day, the sun emerged. Howling racists were becoming thin on the ground. We regrouped, meeting some stragglers who'd tried to reach the National Party march itself. This lot were still up for a fight, claiming that a mob of racists were heading for the park. As the police were occupied with herding the demonstrators into the park, we were able to organise and tool up with stones, bottles, half bricks without drawing attention to ourselves. We never bothered to enter the park itself, waiting outside for the Master Race. Our vigil was not the longest of its kind, and soon a couple of hundred meatheads poured from around a corner, lobbing bricks over the park railings. One missile hit an asian woman in the face. A cheer went up from their ranks at this glorious act of unbridled heroism. I noticed that most of this crew were kids, in their mid-teens with a smattering of older lads with skinhead barnets. This was a primitive collection, some togged up in dated bonehead apparel, to boot. Kids they may have been for the most part, but they were dangerous for sure, some maybe packing blades. We didn't hesitate, launching ourselves full pelt at the fuckers. Having the numerical advantage, they stood their ground for a few seconds. However, a shower of well aimed bricks and bottles, many finding their target, soon persuaded the whole pack to leg it. We didn't bother to give them a hiding, instead we ran parallel to them, lobbing our ammo to deadly effect. A handful of police tried in vain to prevent us from pursuing the übers any further. They were thrust aside in a bedlam of stone striking cars, glass, pavement and thick skulls. Caught up in the excitement I yelled, "EAT THIS!" as I heaved a chunk of concrete at the retreating nazis. Ready to let fly with my remaining bottle, I found myself grabbed by a young copper. "Drop that! You're under arrest!" I instantly pulled myself away, glaring at him in the midst of the chaos. We both realised he was alone, vulnerable, none of his colleagues anywhere to be seen. I smiled, giving him my best twisted grin.

"You've got to be fucking joking, 'aven't you?" He relaxed his already weakened grip encouraged by half a dozen who'd broken off from pursuit of the racists. The young, obviously very recent graduate of Hendon vanished as quickly as he'd arrived. Sensible. We didn't fancy straying much further from the park. Never knew what might be lurking around the corner. An army of heavy dads perhaps.

Later on, collar up, shades on, I departed. On the short, dangerous walk to the tube I passed all sorts of mini-dramas acted out on the pavements. People arguing, scuffles between asian youth and boneheads, a few police trying to contain the still volatile situation. I noticed a violent confrontation at the head of the stairs as I boarded the tube. It looked nasty, a knives and broken bottles job. Asian versus white youth. I was glad to be heading home, back to the centre of town and civilisation.

Next morning, I sat in a café with a mate, reading the papers over a greasy breakfast. A young racist had been stabbed, killed in a fight near the tube. I wondered if I'd witnessed the makings of his demise. Could have been me, anyone, lying on the slab. Just tough luck. Then I read accounts of the National Party rally where their leader was asked by a heckler in the crowd, "What about the killing of that asian lad in Southall last week?" to which he'd replied to cheers, "One down, one million to go!" So much for the moderate, 'populist' image. I leaned over to my fellow diner, "That cunt is as responsible for the death of that kid yesterday as the person who stabbed him." The leader found himself up on charges relating to his outburst, but was later found 'not guilty', the judge using the opportunity to literally wish him well. Despite this ringing endorsement the National Party, not long after the Newham demo, collapsed into its own arsehole, into well deserved oblivion. This left the field clear for the National Front.

CHAPTER 15

The National Front had obviously developed a rather effective method of publicity, recruitment and growth with its ploy of standing candidates in parliamentary by-elections. So in a mirror image tactic, the largest party on the left, the Socialist Workers' Party entered the electoral circus. The Front gained votes from mainly white working class dickheads, whilst the left, mainly down to their anti-racist stance scooped up their comparatively pitiful share from the black and asian community.

The next round of this charade was up in the Midlands, Walsall. I decided to travel up on the spur of the moment when I heard that the Front were having a march in support of their candidate. So on a dismal rainy Saturday I set out alone on a day return, to the gloom of the Black Country, gazing through the windows at the outskirts of a flooded Birmingham. It didn't take long to find the anti-nazi demo, but it appeared to be more of an election roadshow for the SWP. One saving point was that I met up with a large anarchist crew from that neck of the woods. They were well up for it, and it seemed that they'd had plenty of experience rucking with the nazis. If only we in London could have produced such a mob, I thought. Despite our best efforts, we were unable to discover the location of the NF march, so we contented ourselves with shuffling alongside the anti-nazi march, exchanging views, experiences and phone numbers. The anti-nazi demo degenerated into a mere SWP recruitment parade, loudhailers blaring, "SMASH THE NATIONAL FRONT! VOTE SOCIALIST WORKER!" Some of the lads from the SWP with whom I'd been involved in previous brawls against the fascists were clearly embarrassed as the soggy cavalcade wound its way through empty streets, rain pissing down. As the SWP wanted its militants to remain on the march indulging in respectable canvassing, they had no intention of getting anywhere near the Front. This led to some serious frustration amongst their rank and file. I didn't think they were really getting their message over. As I stood on the pavement a man strode out of his house remarking to me, "Is this the lot that like the nig-nogs?" before walking through the acid rain back to his bunker.

Once the march finally halted for what was in effect an election rally for the SWP, their militants felt absolved from any further party responsibilities and went off with us in search of the Front. Having heard something about a place named Bloxwitch, we hailed an empty bus. The driver, a Brummie through and through was only too pleased to take us to our destination. He rolled up the indicator to say "OUT OF SERVICE" and set off at speed. This grand gesture made up for the boredom so far.

We drove for a while, a distance that we'd certainly never have covered on foot, and eventually the rear of the NF march came into view. Thanking the driver, we all leapt off into fairly well-appointed lower middle-class suburbs. A couple of dozen locals had been giving some grief to the Front and were glad of our forty plus reinforcements. Loudhailers were blasting, "VOTE FOR CHARLIE PARKER – YOUR NATIONAL FRONT CANDIDATE." Drawing level to the march I couldn't contain myself, shouting, "I'm never listening to Be-Bop ever again." A bunch of older geezers who must have been jazz fans laughed from the sidelines, a couple joining in, hurling abuse at the fascists. But we'd arrived too late for any real fun, catching only the tail end of their march. They halted, filing into a hall for their rally. Rain lashed down, and the streets were deserted apart from the police who began to move us on. We dispersed, heading for the train station. To my mind, the journey had only been worthwhile because I'd met the Midlands Anarchists who were such a refreshing change from the 'anti-sexist', and 'support-armed-struggle-everywhere-else-in-the-world-but-don't-throw-bricks-at-the-police' brigade back in London.

In this, as in other elections, the Front polled a respectable vote, numbering in the thousands, whilst the left trailed in with their usual Raving Loony result. The absurdity of it all was only compounded when their pitiful result was split as rival leftist sects stood against each other on identical platforms. This was no way to tackle the Front as many in the SWP realised. But as good party members they kept their views strictly to themselves. The SWP leadership were fairly pleased however, because in darkest, dankest Walsall they'd created a new branch. Big fucking deal.

CHAPTER 16

The Front decided to up the ante with a provocative march in north London, to be held at the end of April 1977. This so called 'St George's Day' march was, by another of those strange coincidences the date of Hitler's birthday. But a march to celebrate that auspicious occasion wouldn't have gone down very well, so these home-grown goose-steppers preferred to give it a more 'patriotic' gloss.

At long last, however, our efforts over previous years were bearing fruit, and a handful of us true enthusiasts from the anarchist spectrum had finally succeeded in persuading a sizeable minority that it was well worth taking on the Front. And the police. Of course the usual do-nothing purists continued spewing out their bile. We were as bad as the nazis. Our insistence on aggro was 'macho' and therefore sexist. Police and nazis were human beings, and maybe even the fucking police horses as well. But were we? I had the distinct suspicion that these middle-class gentry considered us fiery hooligans to be lower on the evolutionary scale than the übermenschen. For apparently, we 'ought to have known better'. And so it was, with the prospect of a violent mass-confrontation in the offing an epidemic of childminding broke out amongst the middle class 'non-sexist' anarchists. The irony of course was that if such actions subsequently turned out to be successful, there'd be no shortage of these same goons queuing up to intellectually jerk-off over them, especially for the benefit of visiting foreign comrades who'd be left with the impression that it was these tossers who'd been at the front line of resistance against the fascist tide. But at least we'd reached a point where it was becoming obvious, even to the most blinkered politicos that the Front was growing at an alarming rate, their racist message resounding deep within sections of the working class.

On the tube travelling up to Turnpike Lane I discussed the day ahead with the assembled grouping. Most appeared sceptical, even though we were travelling en masse from a dull early morning picket involving an unrelated issue. Perhaps they felt we should be doing something more important. A couple of us aficionados begun to lose patience: here it was, all on a plate and they were beefing about the set-up. And besides even if we were wrong, there were another 364 days for their pitiful 'Autonomous Actions' the vast majority of which failed even to materialise. Semantics aside, at least we were on our way, and this day as it turned out would prove a real education for most of them.

Reaching our destination, we tumbled out, most bunking their fares. A seething mass of people greeted us, hemmed in by hundreds of police, Special Patrol Group much in evidence. Most of the assembled were some shade of leftist or other attempting to reach the official counter-demo. I avoided them, weaving around to the edge of Ducketts Common. Here the Front were gathering, affording spectators the usual contrast between the impressive forest of flags and the shabby lowlife gathered beneath. Heavy policing meant that we were unable to get anywhere near the bastards. Nearby, on the opposite side of the common, the same old marching-off-in-another-direction counter-demo, comprising the standard collection of soft left, hard-boiled left, Labour Party, local trades union branches, councillors, and even the mayor in all his regalia. Ducking out of that dreary scene, having lost my travelling companions somewhere on the way, I slipped through to the junction of the High Road and Westbury Avenue. I'd calculated that the Front march would strut off in the direction of Wood Green. And nor was I particularly concerned to have ditched the anarchos as I was soon rubbing shoulders with some of the more volatile elements and individuals I knew from various lefty outfits, most notably the SWP a small number of whose members had jettisoned party discipline and were willing to have a go rather than flog papers on the pathetic anti-nazi demo. I'd already been on a more than nodding acquaintance with some of these tasty characters over the years, where it counts; at the sharp end of things. And despite their crap politics, all were genuinely alarmed at the rise of the Front. More importantly, they'd steam in, party orders notwithstanding.

So we gathered in strength at the crossroads, barely contained by the pigs until we began to spill into the road. Now the cops swarmed in, sheer numbers of the stroppy bastards preventing us from reaching our quarry. Unlike many previous confrontations large numbers of local youth, in particular blacks and Greeks had turned out. Some Saturday shoppers even joined in. Certainly we were all determined, ready for the aggro. Some thought that the police would divert the Front march. Were that the case, we'd dive down the side streets, leading part of the crowd to the desired, long-overdue confrontation. But as it turned out the cops were determined to box us in, meaning no diversion. The pigs had by now formed up both sides of the High Road.

Many of us gathered ammunition. Wood from abandoned placards, bottles, fruit and veg distributed by sympathetic shoppers. Police activity hotted up. In the near distance Union Jacks approached in formation, the sound of the drum corps striking up. We all struggled forward, kicking, punching into police lines. Helmets flew, bottles smashed. The fighting raged as the head of the nazi column reached the crossroads. The cops couldn't make many arrests as they were too busy struggling to contain our crowd which, including spectators, numbered about a thousand. As the head of the march drew parallel to the heaving mob, we pelted them with our ammo. The marchers were protected by even more cops, marching at both sides of their demo, obscuring our view of the flag-bearers and drummers. Smashing though the static pavement cop lines, the more violent elements of the crowd – mostly local youngsters plus us aggro merchants – got through to the inner core of police protection. A variety of munitions, including shoes from outdoor display racks flew into the march that buckled but didn't break thanks to the large reinforcements of SPG. I managed to get in real close, cracking a fascist in the chops with a length of broken banner pole. Should have stabbed him with the sharp end as I couldn't really fit in a decent swing. Nevertheless, adequate contact was made, though it failed to deck the cunt. I became detached from the main body of attackers then noticed, by way of a lucky glance, an inspector pointing at me, barking orders: "Nick him! Arrest that man!" Half a dozen SPG swarmed through the mêlée and I flew, sucking in and out of the confusion into the jam-packed traffic ahead. Still the fuckers came for me. They had their truncheons out. I didn't fancy a taste of these. Arrested, and a doing over into the bargain. No thanks. Hundreds of people had spilled out onto the road, providing me with some cover, so I jumped onto a standing bus, rushing up to the top deck. For a quick exit you can't beat a Routemaster. The SPG had lost sight of me, and it gave me great satisfaction to watch them dashing by. I was safe. Passengers on the bus were spitting out of the top deck windows onto the Front and pigs below, shouting insults as they passed. The nazis may well have been gaining support, chalking up respectable votes, but here at least was evidence that their very success was attracting increasing opposition.

I sat down, gasping for breath, then decanted with a couple of the more volatile passengers to bother the rear of the nazi march. Hundreds of us followed them along hurling abuse and the odd missile. The forces of law and order were content now to let us tag alongside, shouting our slogans and curses. The back of the march appeared to contain local supporters and members of the public, and this lot didn't mind reciprocating our threats and verbal aggro. Many, though, appeared to be shitting bricks, taken aback by the size and the fury of the opposition. Neighbours traded threats. No doubt that evening and beyond would be tense, brawls spilling over garden walls, onto the pavements after last orders. I found myself in the company of a few anarchos along with a smattering of leftists. We maintained a constant barrage of verbals, little of it sophisticated: "Come on you nazi cunts! Come over 'ere! Away from police protection, lets 'ave it out. Me 'n' you!" The Fronters responded with their usual opprobrium, "RED SCUM! RED SCUM!" "GO BACK TO RUSSIA!" As the march progressed both sides consolidated. We still picked up support, people coming straight out of their homes to join us. Police were now attempting to walk alongside us but it was a sporadic effort compared with the tight formation shielding the Front. We were content to settle for chanting on the hoof, exchanging the usual classics: "THE NATIONAL FRONT IS A NAZI FRONT..." The übers, plucking up courage responded, "IF IT'S BLACK, SEND IT BACK! IF IT'S WHITE, IT'S ALRIGHT! IF IT'S RED, SHOOT IT DEAD!"

I was joined by Hoxton Rosie, his scarf pulled up over his face. "How many on the Front march?" I asked.

"Just under a thousand, maybe less, maybe more."

But despite these numbers he didn't seem too glum. The reaction against the nazis in an area perceived to be sympathetic to their nonsense had been fantastic, and the day wasn't over yet. We'd long passed Wood Green junction, making our way towards Edmonton. I noticed that our ranks were thinning, and the police in turn were becoming more confident, more aggressive as their reinforcements gained the upper hand, pushing us back. Some ducked off down side streets, hoping to confront the nazis later. I decided to quit whilst ahead, not wanting to meet up with those SPG who may have been redeployed further ahead. So me and Rosie turned around, walking back towards Turnpike Lane along with numerous stragglers. We were greeted with cheers and thumbs-up by some residents once it became apparent we were anti-fascist.

"Rosie, me old son," I asked him, "What d'you think of the day's doings?"

More animated than usual, he turned towards me. "Next time, we've gotta get all our mobs together, give 'em a right fucking hiding. There's no point pissing about, it's now or never."

I knew what he meant, feeling exactly the same myself. This day had been brilliant but we needed more people willing to fight rather than just march under the faded banners of the left. Next time…

Back at Turnpike Lane road sweepers were out, clearing up the mess. Knots of people stood around, deep in conversation, discussing the events of just over an hour ago. There was an air of celebration. We'd stood up to the bully boys, cops and nazis, and had given them a right old fright. The Front certainly wouldn't be back here in a hurry. Rosie met up with a nearby supermarket manager he knew when we popped into a nearby shop for some snout. He was in despair. He'd lost all his Saturday staff. They'd run out, joined the fray, and most hadn't returned. "I've a good mind to dismiss the lot of 'em!"

Rosie wasn't having any of it. "Give 'em a bollocking, fair enough, but don't sack 'em. They were good boys and girls, you should be proud of 'em mate!"

We hung around for a while, occasionally accosted by strangers, many in a state of excitement, all approving of the day's rebuff to the Front. No sign of the 'official' counter-demonstrators though. I later set off home, tired but happy. An evening in for once. There'd be time aplenty to discuss the ramifications of this day, plan the next phase. I was confident I'd now have the majority of the younger elements on board, some were as hooked on the emerging aggro as I was. We wouldn't, I suspected, have long to wait until the cataclysmic showdown, which truth to tell all sides were eagerly awaiting. Us, Front, and police.

CHAPTER 17

Pressure was on the increase as the übermenschen gained support, with even some minor electoral near-misses. In Deptford, south London, the only thing that prevented a nazi councillor from being elected was a split fascist vote between the National Front and the National Party. Meanwhile, for political activists the emphasis had shifted to the cosier, more comprehensible world of industrial dispute, the focus of struggle at the time being the dispute over union recognition at Grunwicks, a firm in northwest London. Many people, trade unionists and others, gave up a day's pay to participate in the mass pickets, attempting to prevent strike-breakers from getting bussed into the premises. The Labour government responded, drafting in an army of police reinforced by our chums, the proto riot squad SPG. Despite frequent clashes and thousands on the picket line, the police succeeded day after day, week after week, in keeping the factory open. The mass pickets became a sort of lefty Ascot with every shade of Leninism on parade. But despite the best efforts of our revolutionary vanguard plus the thousands of burly trade unionists present, the cops always had the upper hand. No barricades were constructed, and nor were the police bombarded with anything more deadly than moronic chants of, "THE WORKERS, UNITED, WILL NEVER BE DEFEATED!" Nearby garden walls that could easily have been turned into ammo were left intact. In other words, day in, day out we were treated to the same old heaving mass frottage with the uniforms. Lobbing anything but dreary slogans would result in the parting of the Red Sea, the hapless chucker being instantly lifted, as trade unionists and leftists stood about muttering their favourite mantra "Provocateur." Of course they knew better. Spineless cunts.

In conversation on the fringes of the picket and in surrounding streets, irritation, frustration, was becoming increasingly evident, especially amongst us sundry miscreants. Salvation was at hand however, though not for the Grunwicks workers, whose tinpot boss with a little assistance from the Met had beaten the entire trade union movement hands down. No, deliverance for us came in the form of a tiny newspaper article. A mere footnote. The National Front were planning another 'March Against Muggers' in Deptford, Saturday 13th August. Needless to say, even on the picket line at Grunwicks, the talk for us was of elsewhere. A full scale riot would be guaranteed because we'd go for it, one hundred percent. The only positive result to emerge from the Grunswick dispute was that it brought us malcontents together, allowed us an opportunity to plot.

A few of us decided to meet up the night before the march to plan the finer details of our intervention. This was on top of weeks of agitation. I'd been hard at work, unofficially liaising with people I knew on the left who'd be up for it, along with the usual host of anarcho ne'er-do-wells. Above a kosher slaughterhouse near Petticoat Lane, chickens squawking as they were decapitated on the chopping blocks below, we gathered. The days were long gone when a couple of enthusiasts would gather only to moan about the lack of interest in anti-fascism in the general scene. Now about thirty hardened troublemakers pored over maps of the Deptford area, pointing out where the nazis would be vulnerable to attack. This, for sure, would be the biggee. A consensus of sorts was reached. Along with militant elements of the crowd, we'd smash our way through police lines, employing force. Failing that, we'd outmanoeuvre the bastards, slipping around their static lines. We'd be tooled up too. No pissing about on this occasion. One stray mystic wondered what we'd do once we reached the Front march, speculating, "Maybe we should try talking to them." Initially a source of great merriment, this bizarre intervention did cause some to become more reflective. "People might be killed..." But for me there could be no backsliding now. As a veteran of sorts I felt entitled to soapbox a little. "Yeah, there's no doubt it'll be a riot. People may get hurt, but we'll smash the nazi scum for sure. They've got it coming and tomorrow's our day!" I assured any waverers that it wouldn't be a matter of us alone. There'd be thousands on the streets, that much I knew from weeks of agitation. We'd only be a component of the action, an important one, but not leading it like some self-appointed vanguard. Here, we were merely going over the possibilities – the possibilities that arise when people in their thousands take to the streets, with determination, sick to death of the stinking fascists. "This won't be another miserable Grunwick fiasco, the cops'll get what's coming to 'em as well." There would be around five thousand pigs on duty. It wouldn't be a walkover. An occupation of New Cross Road near Goldsmiths College had been urged to prevent the nazis from marching beyond their meet-up point in Achilles Street. A nearby corner would serve as the rendezvous point. My humble estimation was for a turnout of at least three to five hundred.

Later in the pub I briefed those from out of town regarding the situation in Deptford. Black and asian families terrorised, firebombings, racist attacks, regrettable support from the white working class for the fascists, racist cops fitting up black youths for 'muggings'. The area had become a nazi Mecca with fascists streaming in from all over London. Such was the combustability of the situation that cops had even moved on charity workers collecting for leprosy victims because, it transpired, some brainless locals took offence at the depiction of African sufferers on their collection tins. I could have extemporised at great length on such matters, but this was a night for resting up. I had an important date the following afternoon, and needed my wits about me.

CHAPTER 18

A chilly damp grey day greeted us as we travelled down to Lewisham. Only a couple of us diehards were making the morning journey to the trade union, soft left counter-demonstration, hoping somehow that we might succeed in diverting a few people to New Cross. That's where we'd need thousands to block the road, hold back the cops, then launch an all out attack on the Front. Halfway to Lewisham the streets appeared remarkably empty, the omnipresent police vehicles aside. Miserable weather seemed to have dampened people's enthusiasm, the usual crackling tension was strangely absent. Still, it was early, any action would be later in the day. So we walked briskly to the park where the counter-demo was assembling, its stewards busily plotting the most direct route away from the nazi gathering and any worthwhile action. A small bottle of brandy had been acquired, just a little something to banish the morning chill, to help energise. I usually adhered to a strict rule of never going into aggro unless completely straight, no blur; adrenaline providing me with buzz enough. And anyhow, you can get as pissed or zonked as you like later. But on so cold a morning, a couple of neat gulps didn't go amiss.

A reasonable number had assembled for the counter-demo. Our instincts told us that a fair few of these were out for confrontation, and had come here mistakenly thinking that the demo would be heading up to New Cross. We hastily conferred, arriving at a decision to join the demo if necessary, and try to divert it up to New Cross. With five thousand police on duty we'd need as many bodies as possible. A determined group of about fifty of us gathered, most of whom I'd met on previous occasions, including some from the SWP who'd sensibly dumped their comics to keep their hands free for action. Gauging the reactions of those we'd already agitated, we concluded that substantial sections of the crowd were up for major aggro. The idea developed to seize the initiative as soon as the demo left the park. We'd split off, taking a sizeable chunk with us. Lacking a loudhailer for communication, it became a case of circulate, mingle, verbalise, persuade. Not that we needed to do much of that. The mood of most, party and union hacks aside, was business-like: this was the opportunity to finally get to grips with the nazis rather than echo empty chants down empty streets, to really do it in a set-piece confrontation. "We're gonna 'ave 'em, and now!" was a fair summary of the general feeling.

Finally the demo, now several thousand strong, left the park, headed by local notables in suits and, leading his flock, an ecclesiastical gentleman in all his gear, mitre included. "It's da bishop!" joked one character, drawing laughter from our subversive throng. As soon as we hit the road we swung into action urging people up to New Cross. "The time for marches is over! Let's go occupy the road up at New Cross!" "Nazi scum this way!" pointing in a general direction up the hill. Most responded immediately, whilst only a couple of years earlier we'd have been rebuffed by the vast majority. But things had now changed, people were eager to get stuck in. The demo was poorly policed – they obviously hadn't expected trouble from this quarter – whilst stewards were virtually non-existent. An ideal scenario. Pavements and road were crowded with people ready for the journey to New Cross, so without further dawdling, off we moved. We probably numbered well over a thousand. Still, no cops, except for a handful in the distance, frantically radioing-in reports of the unexpected mob headed for New Cross. Inevitably a hastily formed line of uniforms appeared, impeding progress. Us instigators halted. Some wanted to smash straight through, and although there were only about a hundred cops it would have damaged our momentum. So we decided to ignore them, swerving right down a side street, a slight diversion. The police, orders not forthcoming, couldn't up sticks and pursue us, so discipline in order they stood like a row of dummies as we all vanished elsewhere. Over the heads of the reception committee a police helicopter clattered impotently as we surged through the streets, ready for anything. Apart from anti-fascists, the streets were deserted. We'd outmanoeuvred the authorities so far and it looked like we'd be able to occupy New Cross Road with or without reinforcements. We took a short cut, running full pelt to the meeting point. A couple of thousand had already gathered, surrounded by police, but not too heavily to discourage an occupation of the road. I rushed up to my mob, which was now about three hundred strong. Breathless, gasping for air, I spluttered, "I know it sounds like bullshit, but…"

"Where the fuck have you been?" someone from the previous evening demanded.

True, I had solemnly promised to arrive early. "But," I continued after a well-earned swig from the brandy bottle, pointing up to the chopper, "there's well over a thousand on their way to occupy the road." Then, with some sarcasm, "and what are you lot doing standing around here on the pavement? Why aren't you on the road, blocking it?"

A moment later, right on cue, the cavalry arrived, filling the road. Some had mysteriously acquired weapons; chunks of wood ripped from fences, iron bars from demolished gates, even dustbin lids. The pavement protesters needed no further cajoling, brushing aside disintegrating police lines to take the road, merging with the arriving mob. Rain steadily drizzled but no-one cared. The cops, fearful of being surrounded and attacked withdrew, forming a larger cordon outside the mass. We were all buzzing now, elated that we'd taken the street with such minimal effort. But this was only a beginning. The real work lay ahead. Holding our ground, then kicking, bricking and fighting our way through police lines to give the nazis what was coming to them.

Folk were pouring into New Cross including many black people and youngsters. The crowd in the road swelled as the pavements overflowed. The three hundred or so anarchists with their black flags and banners lent the scene particular visual appeal for me. Most of them were up for real aggro, as were the majority of the crowd who struggled with the lines of police now several deep who fought in turn to contain the still growing crowd. Placards flew through the air, raining down on the police without causing any damage. With a couple of trusted mates I weaved my way up to the front line armed with a thick lump of wood. The crowds were now dense and movement was slow. Truncheons were out, the cops giving as good as they got. One of the bastards tried to crack me over the head, he hadn't seen I was tooled. This gave me cause to whack rather than bung, so I lashed out at him, catching him on the side of the head. As he staggered back, more surprised than hurt, I felt a surge of pure joy and satisfaction. A couple of enraged cops tried to haul me out, but couldn't make any progress due to the sheer pressure of the crowd. They weren't too pleased though, so one struck a man on the noggin as recompense. Just someone who was trapped there, unable to move. I was close enough to hear the truncheon make contact, a distinctive sound like a wooden ball hitting a coconut at the fun fair. Reason deserted me for a few blind moments as I tried to lunge forward, have it out with the filth. Very stupid of me, considering the day's entertainment was only just beginning and I was intending to see it through to its final curtain. In the event, it proved impossible to brawl with the cops as the ebb and flow of the crowd pushed me sideways. So I returned to the horde, most of whom were well prepared for the fray. Stout clubs made of chair legs, broken banner poles, bits of fencing, bottles, the odd half brick or two. It was the revival of a great British tradition, all the implements of a Saturday afternoon riot. And we were well hyped up, certainly this was the biggun. The whole crowd was now raring to go as even more filth appeared in a vain attempt to contain the mob. City of London cops with their distinctive helmets joined the throng, struggling to hold us back with their hard-pressed colleagues. Rain began to fall again, but spirits weren't going to be so easily dampened, the grey skies now adding to the drama, set off by a backdrop of crumbling cinemas, dance venues, grimy pubs, boarded-up shop fronts and tower blocks looming in the distance. Rumours spread like wildfire amidst the chaos and din: thousands were marching up from Brixton to join us; the fascists had bottled it, hadn't shown up; a thousand nazis were assembled just a couple of streets away; there'd been an anti-asian pogrom on the Isle of Dogs; and that hardy perennial, someone had been killed by the police. All totally impossible to verify one way or another.

In a final effort to clear the road, mounted police were deployed. They trotted their animals, nostrils flaring, right to the edge of the mob who stood solid, resisting all attempts to budge them. Foolishly they succeeded only in pushing most of the crowd close to the point where the nazis were assembling. So far I hadn't actually seen a single fascist. It was impossible now to gauge crowd numbers. Four, five, six thousand. More? Who knows? With a couple of hundred people, all of us brandishing weapons, I moved to the right of the heaving masses, towards the point where the nazis were long overdue to emerge. Progress was painfully slow until a great roar went up and I could see, surrounded by a thick cordon of police, the pointed flagpoles of the Front moving like masts in the distance. The party was on.

The entire crowd surged forwards and the police lines broke. People just swept by, pushing hundreds of filth aside. The human tide advanced remorselessly, heads bobbing up and down. In the distance, the air became thick with missiles flying into the Front march. Now we'd broken free and were running. Ahead, more police tried in vain to stem the flow. They lashed out at random with their batons, occasionally dragging away some hapless soul plucked from the fringes of the action. Four or five would escort each arrestee: the cops by now probably figuring it better to arrest someone and fuck off back to the station, away from the action than be trampled by the mob. This was no Grunwicks, and they were shitting themselves. We were now right up, parallel to the Front, the police cordon having disintegrated, the pigs thinking now of their own skin. No slogans, no chanting, just thousands of yelling voices, the sound of bottles crashing into nazi ranks, bricks crunching as they thudded into the road, off the sides of buildings, advertising hoardings, boarded up shops. Whole garden walls were demolished in seconds. We charged the Front, this was the long awaited opportunity and we weren't reluctant to get stuck in. Bricks and bottles raining all around, it was bloody, no holds barred, hand to hand fighting. Although the Front looked like us down to the long hair and combat jackets, some even sporting flares it was obvious who was who. Flying kicks, punches and the clashing of improvised weaponry filled the space around me. A nazi leapt out yelling, "COME ON THEN, YOU RED BASTARD!" We struggled, me slamming him with a lump of wood. He relaxed his grip, someone had bashed him on the side of the skull with a brick. He caught many a boot as he hit the deck, my own included. I had that glorious novocaine feeling above my upper lip. Pure adrenaline, pure violence. A punk grabbed my club and disappeared into the nazis wreaking havoc. Everyone without exception was brawling toe to toe, the road strewn with broken glass, bricks, bits of timber. I joined the general mêlée in the centre of the road, propelled by the sheer momentum of it all, from one punch up to another, cutting my fists, getting kicked, booting back. I was struck on the side of my face, a small trickle of blood ran from somewhere near my ear, I didn't feel a thing however amidst the brick dust and confusion. The police had regrouped, running, batons drawn, to the epicentre of the tempest. Some of us pulled back to the opposite pavement, bombarding those nazis who'd sought shelter in the shop fronts. The deadly hail, mixed with fumes pouring from smoke grenades, ripped into the bastards. There seemed to be plenty of them but they were outnumbered, outclassed, outgunned and outmanoeuvred. We were heaving whole metal dustbins into the Master Race, taking no small pleasure as they clattered into their midst. Many of these Fronters were tough cunts, they stood their ground and traded blows. I was surprised though at how many of these fuckers were middle aged, there didn't appear to be many youngsters left in their now thinning ranks. By this time most of the nazis had run off to preserve their worthless hides. And after ten more minutes that flashed by like seconds, the Front had dispersed, their tattered remnants heading down Deptford Broadway, bound for Lewisham. The cops too had ceded our portion of New Cross Road to the mob, and we were jubilant, celebrating by tearing and burning captured banners. After some whooping and merriment I came to my senses. I'd been punched, kicked and pounded, although after I'd dabbed some of the blood away from my ear I felt fresh and ready for more. Some of us started haranguing the crowd: "Come on, let's get down to Lewisham! Let's finish the bastards off!"

So we left the revellers, picking up discarded weapons. Thankfully, I'd retained my brandy bottle and gulped back a refreshing swig. After all, it looked like being a long, exhausting afternoon. The Front had vanished by now, save for a few nursing wounds, and a couple laying sprawled in the gutter where they belonged. Fighting continued to rage on the edges of the impromptu carnival, truncheons were still out as knots of young blacks and asians fought the cops. Normally this would have been an exciting conclusion to the day, well worth getting stuck in, but I felt this was a mere diversion, there was still fun to be had. Not worth getting embroiled. So picking up a few stragglers who were up for more, I by-passed the drama at New Cross, dashing towards Lewisham Way, hoping to make it to the High Street. Others were of a like mind, a steady stream of us drifting downhill. No more police impeded our relentless progress. We were all mega-hyped, armed and dangerous. It's a steep descent down to the High Street and the panorama unfolded below as we progressed downhill. I pressed ahead, noticing that most of the folk with us now were black and not all of them youngsters. On the other side of the road a dozen beefy middle aged blacks emerged from a minicab firm, some wearing crash helmets, others carrying bin lids like shields. All were tooled up. Things were getting more interesting by the minute.

Arriving at Lewisham High Street, we joined a mob at the clock tower. Despite this being a busy shopping area, apart from anti-nazis the streets were deserted. Only a handful of police could be glimpsed in the distance, leading me to suspect they were concentrating their efforts on protecting the Front march. Possibly the Front were holding their rally, it had been rumoured that their final destination was somewhere in the vicinity. I didn't fancy standing about all afternoon waiting for the nazis to arrive, so we had to take the initiative before some bright spark lefties decided on another march away from our quarry. In response to the red hot rumour that the Front were holding their rally in a nearby bowling alley, we moved as a body. The mob now consisted of black and white in equal measure, and we were in a mean mood. We swept past stationary police buses, cops seated inside and standing on the pavements helpless as we marched towards our goal. Around the side street adjacent to the bowling alley dozens of police linked arms, keeping us from the exits. Maybe the Front were inside or in the car park. A young black kid threw a brick at a few yards range, he couldn't miss. A fat sergeant was hit, square on the knee. He crumpled, his leg unable to support his ugly bulk. Middle aged heavy blacks started slapping the youngster down: "Don't waste ammunition!" I was flush with excitement, remarking, "These guys really mean business!" Armed with half bricks, bottles, assorted offensive weapons, we surged forwards further up, only to run into a blank wall. Shouts went up, "Watch out! Pigs are regrouping! They're going to trap us!" Sure enough, the uniforms were concentrating near their buses. We had no choice but to retreat the way we came. This meant fighting our way through, and everybody steamed in, bombarding the filth with great gusto. Goodbye brandy bottle as I drained the final drop, lobbing it at the cops. Smoke bombs, flares, bricks, bottles fell amongst police ranks. Some cops went down, most retreated, others picked up flares and returned fire. We had to move before they gained advantage, so we pushed forward throwing bricks at close range. Cops lashed out blindly through the now swirling smoke, everyone a target as though we were all guilty of violent behaviour, which doubtless most of us were. Some unlucky individuals were arrested if they hesitated. The smoke was choking and I'd already masked up, using a souvenir torn from a banner captured from the Edinburgh NF – and they have the nerve to bang on about 'outsiders'. I took a few blows as I rushed through the police lines, but it was all perfunctory really as they bounced off my padded jacket. I was soon out of the turmoil, back at the clock tower. What to do now? Most were up for more aggro, and the police – virtually an arm of the Front rather than "workers in blue" as some lefty morons called them – were as good a target as any miserable, stinking nazi. Maybe better. I'd long wanted to take the bastards on properly, like they did everywhere else on the planet. No more of this push-and-shove that the left went in for on their boring, predictable, within-the-bounds demos.

More rumours flew. A mob was attacking the police station. Where was it? Further down the High Street, beyond the bridge. "Well let's fuckin' go! Let's find it and burn it!" We all struck up a chorus of approval, moving off. Wilder elements were bricking vehicles, putting through the odd shop window. No one bothered looting, we had other things on our minds. By chance, or more likely propelled by the logic of my attitude, I found myself with various uncontrollable rogue elements, veterans of previous brawls. We'd connected at the right place, right time. The gang was all here. We streamed down to the railway bridge bricking and trashing en route. We halted just before the bridge to regroup, collect a larger mob. Smoke rose in the distance, probably a blazing vehicle. Good, we'd gone far beyond anything the British mainland had witnessed during a political event for decades. Instinctively we knew it, digging it all the way. Time to press on and kill the Bill. Suddenly, cries of alarm. "Watch out!" "Behind you!" A strange sight, never seen before, another first for the record books. Down from where we'd just come, across the wide road, slowly advancing, a line of police with riot shields. It looked spooky, fascinating even, the whole scene made menacing by blackened skies and the distant plume of smoke. I was with a couple of hardcases who'd moved over from Ulster, so I asked them what they thought of it all as the mob stood momentarily frozen, gawping at this unique sight. "Aww, you get this every Saturday back home when the pubs and betting shops close for the afternoon."

"What do you think'll happen next?" I enquired.

Already a steady stream of missiles were being hurled by the more athletic who were edging towards the shield line. "Shall we join 'em or what?"

"No," came the voice of experience, "They might open up with baton rounds, rubber bullets; Belfast dildoes."

"Fuck me," I said, "Never thought of that... What about gas? Look..." pulling out my improvised facemask. "Am I supposed to soak it in something? Maybe we should all be moving off to attack the cop shop."

But our discussion came to a sudden close. The shield wall parted, the centre evaporating as the cops formed two defensive shells on opposite sides of the road, back up against shop fronts. They'd been attacked from behind, by another mob who swept past in a hail of bricks, joining us. The cops who'd formerly looked like a shapeless black mass, crouched behind their shields, were now all of a sudden to be far thinner on the ground than we'd anticipated. So we held our ground, gathering reinforcements before seeking out the police station. Without warning, a police bus drove through the reforming shield wall, heading straight towards us. Without hesitation we bombarded it with bricks and bottles. It kept coming as we fell back under the bridge. Although there were only around two hundred of us, we were effectively obscured from the cops' view, and it was impossible for them gauge our numbers. And what with the din and echoes emanating from beneath the bridge, the cops must have been having kittens, we sounded like a thousand. The bus halted before us, it appeared empty, only a driver, but he wasn't going any further. Another vehicle, another empty bus drove towards us. We lobbed from the sides and middle of the road, straight ahead, at the windscreen. The driver swerved, windows badly dented, not stopping, trying to mow us down. Somehow he got through, speeding onwards to safety. We were rather disappointed as a police bus, burning under the bridge would have made for a heart-warming sight. Then another vehicle, an SPG van full of pigs. This time success. The windscreen shattered as several bricks landed simultaneously. The van drew to a halt, the driver's head buried in the steering wheel, out for the count, setting off the hooter in a long, continuous wail amplified under the bridge. The SPG didn't jump out to attack us as they usually did. They couldn't as the hail of bricks and stones smashed the windows, denting the bodywork. The back door of the van was yanked open, revealing a heap of semi-conscious pigs. Lucky for them we hadn't graduated to petrol bombs yet. We all pulled back, leaving the bridge and wreckage. None of us knew the exact location of the police station, but we felt it was close.

At the base of a steep hill there stood a crowd of black kids. Beside them a heap of bricks and stones from a road works and a small barricade of traffic cones and planks. We waved over to them, "Where's the police station? We're gonna burn it down!"

"Over there," they gestured, "Keep going."

As if by magic, a group of cops appeared, yelling their heads off. Batons drawn, they ran down the hill to the barricade. From where I was standing they looked quite young, maybe hurried in straight from Hendon. They also appeared leaderless, no portly sergeant or pinch-faced inspector. The kids didn't bottle it, lobbing bricks with great determination. The police charge halted as rapidly as it had materialised, the cowardly bastards turning on their trotters and fleeing back up the hill. Morale it seemed, had collapsed, along with their coordination. But not everywhere. More shouts went up. "Watch out! They're coming through in a convoy of buses!" Sure enough, in the distance, a phalanx of vans spread across the road, creeping forwards, no doubt jam-packed with angry SPG, just aching to wreak vengeance after they'd discovered the carnage under the bridge. Rumours flashed. Some nutter had gained entry to the trashed van, stabbing coppers to death. We were getting thin on the ground and with the massed vans advancing, we melted away, not wishing to be overwhelmed, trapped. We'd have been up for a right old battering and worse, with heavy charges to boot. No point persisting once you've lost momentum. We were miles ahead and it was time to quit.

So we drifted to the nearest train station, whence we hoped we'd find some übermenschen. Waiting around for the customary age we were still animated, finest day ever, the universal sentiment. Didn't know what was best, the nazis or the police getting a hiding.

Our noses glued to the windows, the train departed for the centre of town, the streets below seeming deserted, quite unlike the scenes as we pulled into the next station. Knots of people were slugging it out on the embankments, tracks and adjacent waste ground. Great cheers arose as some of our fellow passengers disembarked, eager to rejoin the fun and games. The next station was entirely populated with battered Fronters who didn't dare board the train. So aside from some shouting and catcalls between carriage and platform, and a few half-hearted missiles bouncing off the side of the train, that was the end of the day's dramatic events. As the train pulled out, we jeered, reminding them one last time of their comprehensive defeat. "And your mates, the pigs got what was coming to 'em n'all!"

Back at Charing Cross, hyped to the nth degree I bade farewell to the Lewisham veterans, convinced we'd given more than a minor jolt to the smug, complacent British body politic. Hopefully we'd set a precedent for the future. Anything would be better than the apathetic crap we'd had to endure up till then. Alighting from the train, an overwhelming racket swamped my senses. I fully expected to be walking into another riot, but instead it was the usual bustle of thousands of shoppers and day-trippers.

The next day's papers were full of the usual hysterical garbage. The pigs, of course, were heroes, hundreds of them having been injured by the mob. So fucking what! A few days later in the centre of Birmingham, the Front held an election meeting. It came as no great surprise when the good citizens of Brum took a leaf out of our book, pelting the police protection with bricks and bottles. Having no riot shields themselves, the police were forced to deploy hastily issued army numbers. Certainly the introduction of riot shields proved we'd raised the stakes a notch or two. Who knew where things could go from here? Much further I hoped. Petrol bombs, barricades, gas, guns, revolt... bring it on!

CHAPTER 19

Things were fairly quiet for a while until another parliamentary by-election loomed early in 1978, this time in the London suburb of Ilford. As the Front were standing a candidate, this would provide another welcome opportunity to give them grief, maybe with the added bonus of putting a few more coppers on the early retirement list. This time, however, the Front couldn't provide the usual focal point for us to launch an attack. Marches were out of the question as the Minister of the Interior, better known by the innocuous-sounding title of Home Secretary, had slapped a blanket ban on all demonstrations in the Greater London area. Obviously they didn't want another Lewisham. So the nazis were reduced to 'mass canvassing'. All the same, us anti-fascists had an incentive to turn up as the Young National Front were putting in a much-heralded public appearance; an opportunity, no doubt, for a constructive exchange of views. Their magazine, a tatty rag by the name of Bulldog was, if such things could be imagined, even cruder in its racist sentiments than the vile National Front News. The football column featured a 'League of Louts' wherein the racist antics of various football supporters were catalogued and celebrated. Top marks were given to those firms who screamed the loudest abuse and lobbed the greatest quantity of bananas onto the pitch whenever a black player was fielded. One moron was showered with hearty congratulations for having hurled a coconut. It's a wonder they weren't plucking off their thick heads and tossing them onto the pitch.

So on yet another cold, grey winter's afternoon, we headed out, this time down Ilford way. The whole event turned out to be an exercise in frustration, police everywhere guarding small clumps of nazis, roaming groups of anti-fascists, preventing any physical confrontation between the contending factions. The group of hooligans with whom I wandered the area was trailed by police in vans. After a couple of hours of this bullshit, it was time to cut our losses, walk back to the tube. A small group of Jewish lads, distinguishable by their Star of David jewellery beckoned, "Oi, come here, have a word." I went over, thinking maybe they'd mistaken us for Front, to smooth things over if need be. But no need. "You an' your mates fancy a crack at the Front?" Of course, but how? There were hundreds of cops guarding the bastards, the streets otherwise empty but for nazis, cops and a dwindling collection of folk from the recently formed Anti Nazi League, who weren't really up for much. However, good news. "You won't believe it mate, there's a group of YNF standing outside the police station and it's the only place around here where there's no Old Bill hanging around!" Too good to be true? Maybe, but well worth checking out.

Sure enough, just around the corner, not a cop in sight, the young apes. Without hesitation we crossed the road shouting friendly greetings. It wasn't until the trusty steelcaps and swinging fists went in that they cottoned on we weren't Fronters ourselves. It didn't take long to finish them off, leaving them battered and splattered all over the pavement. After shaking hands with our new-found friends, we fucked off.

Waiting for the tube I was accosted by one of those anarchist bearded wonders, all bottle-bottom glasses and anti-sexist platitudes. "Are you responsible for what happened outside the police station?"

A normally modest chap, I was on this occasion rather pleased with myself: "Yeah, well, I was in on it."

"Well," he spluttered, full of self-righteous indignation, "I think it was disgusting, you never gave them a chance. Just kicked them senseless as they lay on the ground, helpless."

My temper almost overflowed to the point of thumping him. "Look cunt, that's how we deal with 'em. That's that. No apologies." Adding, "And besides, if they had their way you'd be first up the chimneys."

He sloped off, revolted, poor gentle soul. He'd probably later relate to some equally middle-class feminist what a brutal, sexist, violent, irrational, almost fascist pleb I was. I was glad to be of unintentional service, providing the likes of him with an opportunity to demonstrate how kind, meaningful, non-violent they were. Queer chat-up lines, but apparently effective in those rarefied circles. Not that I really gave a toss, living as I did in a permanently aggravated haze. What I found far more frustrating was reading the newspapers the next day. That very Saturday, whilst we'd been dodging around Ilford, in Italy thousands of schoolkids had taken to the streets armed with petrol bombs demanding the abolition of examinations. Why not here? What was the matter with this dull country and its apathetic inhabitants? Still, Lewisham had shown what was possible. But was it just a flash in the pan?

It did seem, at least on a street level, that the fascists were in retreat. Apart from in certain well-defined strongholds, every time they dared venture out they were in danger of extreme physical opposition. Many youngsters who'd otherwise have been tempted to join the Front on their inner-city jaunts came over to our side. Put crudely it's better, more fun, to lob bricks and bottles at the police lines than to hide, cowering behind them. Believing the political and social atmosphere to finally be thawing somewhat, I started hinting at another agenda, something that had been swirling about in my dissatisfied imagination since my mid teens. Why, if we've gained control of a small area, even if only a handful of streets for a few hours should we voluntarily relinquish them? Why not try to kick off something bigger, better, with unlimited potential? I never tired of repeating my favourite mantra: to our eternal shame the entire population had sat on its arse in 1968, content to still be celebrating England's World Cup victory of two years previous. Whilst Europe and vast stretches of the globe were in upheaval, Britain remained a bastion of dull conformity and reactionary crap.

After the joys of Lewisham, the Anti-Nazi League and Rock Against Racism had taken off big-style, rallying tens of thousands of young people to the anti-fascist cause. The gang of malcontents I hung around with, all chafing at the bit, crying out for nothing less than mass urban revolt were of two minds about this development in anti-fascism. For one thing, the ANL was basically a coalition of hard and soft leftists and liberals of various persuasions, the very creeps who've always help hold us back from anything interesting. Politically it was very dubious, little more than a machine for sucking up to and recruiting votes for the Labour Party in the forthcoming general election. As far as I was concerned successive Labour governments had maintained, encouraged the conditions that allowed the fascists to thrive and Labour were part of the festering heap of garbage that would have to be swept away. On the plus side, tens of thousands of previously apathetic young people had committed themselves to coming out onto the streets in opposition to nazis and racism. Nothing wrong in that. Question was, where would all this unleashed energy go?

In a modest fashion political history was made on Sunday April 30th with the Carnival Against the Nazis that gathered at Trafalgar Square, destination Victoria Park, Hackney. Here there would be a music festival with bands such as the Clash, X-ray Spex, Steel Pulse and the Tom Robinson Band. I don't know how many punters they were expecting, but the ANL, the fifty-seven varieties of leftism, in fact everybody, was astounded by the turnout. Umpteen thousands crammed the streets prior to marching to Victoria Park, mostly people in their under thirties, all races, large numbers of working class youth from the estates. Indeed, by any criterion, this was impressive. Of course the left were present in all their various insidious forms, but they were heavily outnumbered by human beings. The youth were exuberant, not interested in building up a Leninist, Bolshevik, Trotskyite party circa 1917. This must have been a grave disappointment to the SWP who'd invested a great deal in the ANL. Still, the remoras of revolution would have plenty to latch onto and feed off over the next couple of years.

The great mass set out from the square just after midday, an endless stream of humanity. After standing around observing this with a gang of troublemakers, some of us decided to avoid the long slog and shift ourselves down to Brick Lane where the nazis were gathering. Sure enough, a couple of hundred of England's finest idled, probably expecting the usual shambling leftist demo. They were fairly vocal when the head of the march appeared, but were soon reduced to impotent grunts and placard waving, protected by a large body of the boys in blue. So we departed, heading down to the park. Some of us were well steamed up, expecting trouble. We'd come psychologically prepared for aggro, anything from a massive punch-up to barricades. Rumours were circulating, but the SWP and assorted goons didn't want the situation to get out of control. After all, one didn't want to damage the chances of Labour being re-elected did one? Arriving at Victoria Park, I'd come to some definite conclusions. This ANL phenomenon had umpteen dangers and contradictions, channelling healthy street violence into acceptable modes of protest, alternative consumerism and the deadly embrace of Labour; the Trots gleefully scooping up any detritus. As we stood about at the entrance to the park, us miscreants barracked the leftists, much to their obvious annoyance. Some hotheads wanted to invade Hoxton, attack the nazi's watering holes, their leaders' cave dwellings, dish out the same treatment they'd been delivering to the helpless over the years. The numbers were present, but were they willing? Apparently not. Crap music being more far more important. The organisers even refused to announce from the stage that at that very minute, only a few miles away, the Front were holding a May Day march, let alone its assembly point and destination. Keep it all within the bounds of respectability. Consume. Go home. Vote Labour. The atmosphere prevented anything interesting developing, so we resigned ourselves to puffing joints, downing overpriced booze, eventually drifting off. Deep down inside, I wasn't surprised that so many had turned out that day to explicitly support the ANL. Many had signed up and joined. My hope was that the street activists who'd been opposing the fascists physically wouldn't be sucked into this vortex of respectability masquerading as militancy. I wanted the more volatile elements currently drawn to the ANL to throw aside the leadership, carry on with the task of smashing the nazis and racists, then onwards to the real enemy, the forces of law and order. Let's face it, by now some of us troublemakers were regarding opposition to the nazis as an excuse to riot and attack the police; something that was an anathema to the left who merely wanted everything under control so they could pursue their discredited goals of party-building, tailing the unions and Labour onwards in the great project of endlessly reproducing the decades-old dull conformity of British politics. The same old bollocks.

CHAPTER 20

Another by-election, another blanket ban on demonstrations in the Greater London area issued by our wonderful Labour government. The Front were to hold an election meeting in a school building, however. This time, south of the river, Brixton to be precise. I was sadly aware that there'd be no chance of storming the building, or even of laying it under heavy siege. The will to do so had been dissipated amongst the majority of activists. They'd been sucked into the ANL, and with a General Election looming many felt that another Lewisham-type affair could jeopardise the chances of Labour holding on to power. I couldn't give a toss about Labour, remarking, "Riots will be better under the Tories." The school building would be guarded by a small army of police. I knew that the chances of a clash were miniscule, that this would likely be another ritualised stand-off. However, we could always get lucky.

On that pleasant warm Saturday afternoon it was somewhat disturbing to see the local population by and large unperturbed by the mini-drama enacted in their side streets. Mostly ANL and lefty types had turned out, the local black population ignoring the presence of hundreds of fascists bused into the area, an attitude I found puzzling. The main protest was at the rear of the school building, anti-nazis hemmed in by police. Same old collection of lefties sucking up to Labour. "There's a difference between the Labour Party and the Labour government, you know." Yeah, yeah, yeah... This being semi-trendy Brixton there was an unusually large turnout of 'non-sexist' men and their hideous feminist chicks. As me and my compatriots had little desire to mix with such types, it was off to the main entrance and the street opposite in the hope of encountering the odd stray nazi and kindly offer him an enlightening critique of racism and National Socialism. No joy, as the whole area was swamped by countless uniforms and we'd picked up an escort of our beloved SPG. Reined in by cops, we stood around, hands in pockets. Soon, a stir of excitement. In the distance, under police escort, a large troop of Front apes, the heavy mob. The SPG closed ranks, hemming us in further. Not that we'd have risked arrest for a pointless attack. Then, as they drew closer we noticed, head and shoulders above the motley crew, standing over seven feet tall, the Front's legendary 'Incredible Hulk'. I'd heard talk of this creature and this was my first sighting. Jaws dropped, even our own 'Big Boy', our largest tastiest hooligan, all six foot four of him, gasped in amazement. All were flabbergasted. Even the SPG shook their head in disbelief as this carnival of freaks passed by. I dived around the corner with the others to relate the wondrous sight we'd seen, and inform the anti-nazis that the

Front were now inside. I couldn't resist waxing lyrical about what I'd just witnessed. Some of the 'non-sexists' overheard my lurid descriptions and started chanting an incredible slogan at me: "MACHO POSTURING OUT! MACHO POSTURING OUT!" I'd had enough. I could have slapped some of these ponces there and then. Instead I fucked off, leaving our pristine comrades waving their ANL lollipop placards. I could only hope that they'd stumble across the übers later ... in some dark alley perhaps. Then maybe they'd learn the true meaning of macho.

Another ANL carnival was due in September, this time parading from Hyde Park to Brockwell Park near Brixton. Fine, except on the same day the Front were marching in the East End to their new headquarters, a large refurbished building in Great Eastern Street, Shoreditch. The nazis had recovered somewhat from the shock of the first ANL carnival. Racial attacks were once more on the increase, along with arson and extreme forms of harassment. The NF were openly encouraging skinhead gangs, who were currently undergoing a revival, to attack anti-fascist gigs and commit minor and not so minor acts of terror, whilst at the same time denying all knowledge of and responsibility for the resulting intimidation and violence. The ANL were powerless to answer, and the situation was only salvaged by those individuals and groups on the fringes who refusing to be intimidated, were prepared to slug it out in the backstreets with the skins and nazi psychos. Many casualties resulted. It was no surprise then that the ANL ignored the latest NF march. Those of us willing to have a crack were reduced to pleading in Hyde Park, trying to get people to forget the carnival. "Fuck listening to a load of discredited politicians and rock stars trying to build their careers. Come down to the East End. Meet up in Brick Lane, and let's batter the Nazis" But apathy prevailed, and only a couple of hundred left with us for the tube to Bethnal Green. The streets around Brick Lane were deserted. We met with some Asian youth holding that part of the Lane near Bethnal Green Road where we fully expected the Front to go on the rampage. Many police were on duty, although somewhat static, so we moved at will. Even here the ANL mentality seemed to reign, most content merely to wait for the non-existent reinforcements from the carnival. Much more of this and it would have been too late, the Front would have been presented with a walkover in the heart of the East End. A tremendous boost to their morale. As we stood on the corner of the Lane, in an empty garage forecourt, some of us snapped. Despite the fact that I was already facing – amongst others – an assault charge, due up in court in a couple of weeks, I couldn't face standing around any longer. We had enough people to harass the Front march, knew where they were headed, their new headquarters being only five minutes walk away on Old Street. I could well understand the local youth defending their area against any nazi incursion, but the rest were confused, lacked the initiative to take the offensive. A mere handful of us set out, dodging police through familiar side streets, picking up some stragglers on the way. We got within 100 yards of the ape house, police blocking any further progress as the Front march came into view. As there were only about fifty of us, an attack would have been suicidal. One joker suggested an absurd token action, a touch of surreal genius. "Why not just walk out into the road, a dozen of us, and sit down in the middle, right in the path of the demo?" The Front were in a triumphant mood, throaty cries bellowed as they marched through the empty streets past their new building, "IT'S OURS! IT'S OURS!" Good sense prevailed, no invasion of the road. A good kicking followed by a night in the cells wasn't such an attractive proposition. We were eventually pushed back to Brick Lane by aggressive policing. Some of the pigs were mouthing racist garbage, trying to provoke a violent reaction. We rejoined the Brick Lane gathering, ANL and SWP orators spewing out the usual garbage about how the Front had been defeated on this historic day. Such patent nonsense led to severe heckling from those who'd just arrived from Great Eastern Street. It almost resulted in violence as some of the arrogant hacks accused us of being fascist supporters. Some irony here since we were quite clearly in the company of a number of asian lads and lasses. Realising this, they shifted to more familiar territory labelling us 'provocateurs'. Eventually we drifted down the Lane towards Aldgate where, it was rumoured, people were arriving from the carnival to support us. Too little, too late. We'd only gone a couple of hundred yards down the Lane when we were confronted with a freshly painted Neolithic scrawl: "WE'RE BACK! NF RULE!" At Aldgate East tube, militants were pouring from the exits. Most were pissed off as the ANL had withheld information about doings around the Lane. By now, however, the Front had dispersed, no incursions apart from the daubers. Heated discussion followed in the local pubs. Amongst some of the assembled, a seismic shift had occurred in their attitude towards the ANL. Talk was of a more bitter future. Guerrilla actions, hit and run against nazi hangouts. Without the blessed sanction of the Party, a handful had been sporadically doing this form of action for a while already.

CHAPTER 21

On a cold, misty Sunday morning I walked from Highbury to Hoxton via Canonbury. The reason for this chilly stroll was a local ANL demo that would terminate around the Brick Lane area. Here the Front and other nazis had their sales pitch, a gathering of the apes. I was accompanied on this jaunt by a mild mannered but deadly humorous Irish fellow by the name of Ken. He too had become somewhat caustic about the scene from which due to my perceived 'violent' attitude, I found myself being frozen out. Glad of each others company we honed our sarcastic, menacing banter, a light-hearted, if puerile response to our pathetic critics. Pausing for breath outside a typical large Islington town house inhabited by male and female 'anarcha-feminists', the very people who'd caused me so much trouble. As well I knew from being on the receiving end of their rumour mill, innuendo and general poison here lay the enemy within. "They had a party here last night," announced Ken, "Don't suppose you got an invite?"

I shrugged. "Didn't even know about it. Got as much chance of an invite as the Front, probably less. Besides, I never go to parties I'm invited to..."

But deep down I felt resentful as we strolled down to Hoxtonia, musing over the ironies of the situation. Here I was, the ultimate in mindless, sexist thuggery, holding back the Hoxton floodgates, preventing the horrors from spilling over the border into leafy Canonbury. The nazi racist psychos had so far been contained in their little patch of urban jungle, not daring to venture out to terrorise their Commie, Liberal, Pinko betters in Canonbury or Barnsbury. A weird form of class deference. Yet here we were, heading down to Hoxton, bottling up the fascists, indirectly keeping these middle-class areas nazi-free, and when's all said and done, slugging it out with our own class, rather than taking on our oppressors.

I cracked a few lame jokes. "Ken, what's the difference between a sexist man and an anti-sexist man?... An anti-sexist man always cries after he's beaten up his girlfriend."

"Yeah," remarked Ken, saves on the expense of flowers and chocs, and it makes 'em appear meaningful."

"Huh," I snorted, "The cunts." It's a funny old world.

We arrived in not so sunny Hoxton, the anti-fascist demo gathering on the outskirts. I declined to join the head of the march, preferring to observe from the sidelines with some mates. Unlike previous excursions in this neck of the woods, there didn't appear to be any organised opposition, although we knew that the nazis would be waiting at Brick Lane. I stood on a grassy mound in the company of a few brooding locals watching the mist disperse and the march gather. They obviously disapproved of the demo, and not from an ultra-left perspective. They were tight-lipped however, only a couple of old ladies showing any volubility. So I went over for a friendly natter. From my appearance they didn't suspect me of being one of them 'Communists' they weren't so keen on, so they gratefully bent my ear with their concerns about, "All them pakies and blackies mugging old-age pensioners, all the crime they bring to the area."

"Yeah," I mused sarcastically, "Weren't like that in the old days when Ronnie and Reggie were around. Safe to walk the streets, leave your door open, none of this gratuitous violence."

They smiled, one perking up, "That's right son, they were such lovely boys."

I departed, speechless.

The demo moved off, over a thousand strong processing through empty streets. We joined, searching out known aggro merchants we were aquainted with. We noticed fading strings of royal jubilee bunting, 1977 vintage, strung along dismal council flat balconies. Anywhere else it would have been long rotting in landfill sites. Nearing Brick Lane, tension rose. We braced ourselves, but apart from noisy cat-calls directed at us by down-to-earth Eastenders, nothing. One old hag stuck her hair-netted bonce out of a top floor window shouting down at us, "YOU'RE A BLOODY DISGRACE! YOU SHOULD ALL 'AVE YOUR BOTTOMS SPANKED!" A spontaneous cry erupted from assembled jokers, "OOOOOH... YES PLEASE MISSUS!" Police were thick on the ground as we passed Brick Lane via Bethnal Green Road. Around two hundred übers were held in check by the cops, waving placards and Union Jacks, bellowing their usual chorus: "GO BACK TO RUSSIA!" "'AVE A BARF!" "GET YER 'AIR CUT!" Ironic since so many of these fuckheads sported manes and facial fungus that they wouldn't have looked out of place in a sixties love-in. The march continued without hindrance for a boring rally in a park. There was some talk of going back for a scrap with the Master Race, but with so many police around it would not have been a wise move. Instead, we decided to return the following week. No advertisements, just word of mouth. And we knew where to find them.

The week after the anti-fascist march, a crew of us met up outside the boozer on Liverpool Street Station. Most were lefties present were acting independently from their respective parties and organisations that would have objected strenuously to unsanctioned activity. Mixing with people from rival factions? Beyond control? Never. But these folk, many of whom I was on more than a nodding acquaintance with had a different, more immediate agenda from the pointyheads of the central committees. They really wanted to give the nazi scum a good kicking and drive them off the streets, not wave big cardboard ANL lollypops at them. It was time, long overdue, to stop the fascists congregating, stirring it up, unleashing their thugs and boneheads. Race attacks had increased all over East London, resulting in fatalities. The weekly opposition to the National Front Brick Lane paper sale consisted in an ineffectual picket on the opposite side of the road, guarded by the police. At Liverpool Street station, about forty meaty geezers turned up, most of them in a different aggro class from the usual. Meaner and older. After a brief discussion we agreed to rendezvous later about twenty yards away from both nazis and police, ignoring the picket. Off we drifted in twos and threes. A particularly cold morning, we were well wrapped up, looking indistinguishable from the Front, wearing no badges or other means of identification that would allow police or nazis to eyeball us prematurely. With caps and woolly hats firmly planted on our heads, we tried to mingle, under the noses of the Front. There was almost instant recognition from the fascists, after all we'd been having a crack at each other for a long time. As we traded insults, I suspected that somehow they'd gotten wind of our intentions beforehand as plenty of heavies from Hoxton and beyond were lurking. Like our mob, most of them were older geezers, built like dockers with mean, pugilistic expressions. One leading NF heavy had recently been burgled whilst out terrorising those from sunnier climes, the daring thief making off with his precious fishing rod collection valued at hundreds of quid. Bad natured banter ensued. "Oi, Del! Wanna buy some fishing rods!" "Your daft son nicked 'em Del. Inside job. Yeah, took 'em up to Uncle Hymie's shop in Golders Green." The Front were less inventive with their verbals, "FUCKIN NIGGER-LOVERS!" "WE'RE GONNA 'AVE YOU!" Invitations to tango were proffered, the small numbers of police unable to contain the rapidly developing situation. They radioed for urgent reinforcements. "COME ON YOU NAZI SCUM, QUIT MOUTHING IT! LET'S BE HAVING YOU!" The thuggish Del was being restrained by his racial comrades, who suspected a trap as we were so up for it, so confident. The ANL picket stood frozen in disbelief, glad to be tucked behind a thin cordon of police. After this short interlude of verbal jousting, the Front steamed in, a dozen of the most evil looking bastards leading the charge. We all ran automatically to a nearby junction to regroup and grab weaponry from a conveniently placed road works. Only about twenty Front followed hot-foot, the rest of their flotsam held back by the cops. They were probably grateful as they witnessed the toe-to-toe with the now outnumbered fascist heavies. These nazis were game as fuck, seasoned street brawlers, shithouse builds. They decked a couple of our geezers with crunching blows, not bothering to stick the boot in as they pushed forwards. We smacked them with road signs and metal rods. I took a massive blow on the side of my chin, sending me spinning, sickening pain coursing through my head. I felt like I wanted to throw up, so brutal was the shock. I staggered into the road clutching my jaw. Boots went in, glancing off my legs, but I felt nothing.

Acting on sheer animal instinct, as really I ought to have fucked off pronto, I plucked up a traffic cone, wading back in, adrenaline providing instant pain relief. One nazi stood in front of me, his back turned, shouting his head off. "COME ON YOU CUNTS! I CAN TAKE THE LOT OF YOU!" He was small but stocky, his neck the thickness of a man's waist. I swung the cornetto full force, the heavy weighted base landing square on the back of his neck. He grunted, reeled, but never went down. I'd put full force into the blow and only dented the blob. Police arrived, jumping out of their vans. We all departed, making for the Seven Stars in Brick Lane. I downed an uncustomary large number of drinks to help deaden the pain in my throbbing jaw. Much to my embarrassment I found it difficult to sup as I couldn't open or close my jaw without great discomfort, much of the liquid ending up dribbling from my mouth, saturating my clothing. I accepted defeat and went on to shorts. I'd probably sustained a hair-line fracture, because it took a whole fortnight before I was okay again. We could have mustered another crew that afternoon and hit the nazi drinking dens in Bethnal Green Road, such as the foreboding adobe-like structure, the Blade Bone, or the nearby Well and Bucket. The presence of large numbers of police patrolling in vans forced commonsense to prevail, however. We'd suffered plenty of cuts and bruises but the Master Race hadn't come too well out of it themselves. A hard fought score draw was our verdict on the day's play.

CHAPTER 22

Nineteen seventy-nine brought the General Election. The ultimate in boredom for any anarchistic troublemaker, but interesting from the perspective of us anti-fascists as the Front were standing many candidates. So on Friday evening, April 20th, the Front empowered by the 'Representation of the People Act' were allowed to hold a London wide election meeting at Islington Town Hall, London Zoo's monkey house being unavailable. Directly opposite the town hall was the anarchist bookshop, Rising Free, stocked mostly with literature ripped-off from lefty and liberal establishments. Outside, ANL and various anti-fascists swelled the pavements, a noisy but fundamentally peaceful scene. It didn't look like there was going to be any concerted rush on the Town Hall, let alone an attempt to occupy the premises. Although rumours were circulating that anti-nazi hit squads were prowling the streets to pick off stray Fronters, it didn't seem worth the effort from our vantage point in a room above the bookshop. Some of us wanted more than just the opportunity to chin the odd nazi. The usual vast numbers of constabulary were holding back the crowds, parting from time to time to allow the Fronters into the town hall. Despite the infernal din, there was no aggro as the nazis strutted by unmolested. The anti-fascists chanted the same tired old slogans: "NAZI SCUM! NAZI SCUM!" "THE NATIONAL FRONT IS A NAZI FRONT..."

"Yeah, and the pope is a catholic and bears shit in the woods," commented one of our number.

"It's deadly dull, nothing's happening at least 'til the rally's finished. Let's go to the pub," piped up another.

Veteran of many past clashes I knew we'd face hours of waiting with the strong possibility of no aggro at the end. And going into the pub was always a fatal move as you'd probably not emerge until closing time, missing any action outside.

Then one genius had a brainwave: "If it's meant to be a public meeting, why don't we go inside, disrupt it?"

This suggestion hardly met with enthusiasm, the lure of the pub being preferable to suicide. But, oblivious to danger, disappointed with the lack of action, stupid to the point of recklessness, I was game. "Fuck it, I'm going in! Anyone fancy it?" Even though I was in the company of hardened reprobates, hardly anyone considered the proposition. Only two volunteers emerged. A goofy looking geezer with glasses named Gaz and the beefy Big Nose. At least they could handle themselves in a barney, being ex-football hooligans. Off we went. "See yer later folks!"

Gaining admission through the side-entrance would have proved difficult had we crossed straight over Upper Street, crowds and police making that route impassable. However, this was home territory, and it took only ten minutes, a minor diversion through Florence and Seddon Streets before we arrived at the door. Lines of police watched impassively as the Front, overwhelmingly male, sauntered in, unfazed by the nearby hostile reception. They seemed to be in an ebullient, confident mood. No instant entry for our trio, however. We were forced to queue outside by the police who only permitted forty members of the public entry, and then individually or in small groups. We were stared out by NF security as we gingerly walked up the stone steps following a brief wait. But the Good Lord smiled on us tonight. Still, it didn't take great powers of clairvoyance to envisage a later, less dignified descent down these self same steps. As we didn't look like lefties, we had no difficulty gaining entry to the foyer. I'd had the foresight to pin an 'NF – Rock Against Communism' badge to my lapel. So, unrecognised, pondered over by dull intellects, eyeballed by a collection of freaks togged up in ill-fitting suits and bomber jackets we were ushered into the hall.

"Fuckin' hell," I muttered, "We ain't gonna get out of here alive!" The large hall was two-thirds full. Seated on the right-hand side was the most evil looking collection of throwbacks I'd ever seen under one roof. Swelling the crowds of nazis were dozens of postal workers from the nearby sorting office. Before I was even seated I was pointed out by some of the town hall boiler workers from my local union branch.

Instant abuse. "What are you doing here with these stinking nazis?"

"What are you doing here with them dirty reds?"

As they rose from their seats, it seemed like a quick exit, stage left was in order. However, they were urged to remain seated by the fifty or so stewards. "Ignore 'em. We'll deal with 'em later." The stewards formed a cordon between us lucky punters and the über faithful. We found ourselves separated by an aisle filled with these brutes. As we took our seats we cottoned on: the event was being filmed for national TV, so they'd have to be on their best behaviour. At least we'd be relatively safe in the hall. Now I felt relaxed, ready to rock later if need be.

We sat down near the front, next to an alarmed looking asian geezer. "Don't worry mate," I reassured him as we plonked our frames into the chairs, "We're friends. We're here to give it to the nazis."

"Yeah," added Big Nose, "We ain't scared of 'em, they're just a bunch of wankers."

I removed my badge, theatrically spat on it, flicking the object into the massed ranks of Front. This caused a minor ripple but as we suspected, the stewards had the situation well under control. Only about thirty members of the public had been allowed in, selected for their diminutive stature, making them easy meat for the stewards. On the stage was a table decked with bunting, behind which was set empty chairs, ready for the arrival of the silver-backed males. Large Union Jacks on poles formed the backdrop, a couple of which as one wit pointed out, had been hung upside down. Even after all these years I still couldn't tell one way or another.

We were verbally menaced by the stewards, one individual in particular, decorated with tramline scars, leant over to the asian geezer: "If you make so much as a peep, I'll rip your fuckin' paki face off!"

Big Nose grunted back, "Fuck off wanker or you'll get a slapping."

Tramlines slunk off, muttering under his bad breath, "We'll see about that."

Suddenly, drowning out the to and fro of jeers and insults, the strains of 'Jerusalem' crackled over a loudspeaker. Few of the Front appeared to actually know the words, but that didn't prevent them from erupting into a hideous cacophony of Chimpanzee, Gorilla and Gibbon come the final line, "IN ENGLAND'S GREEN AND PLEASANT LAND!"

The show was about to start. Onstage filed the warm-up men, a collection of dishevelled middle-aged men who looked like a line-up of sex-offenders down the local nick. They appeared to be wearing the world's last de-mob suits. We heckled the speakers, surprised as they cracked with ease. They resorted to crude abuse in retaliation. Meanwhile, the stewards were having great difficulty restraining the hyped-up übers who were well pissed off at our interventions. Speaker after speaker reeled as we maintained our verbal onslaught. Distorted reddened faces spat out venom: "YIDDOS!" "RACE TRAITORS!" "NIGGER LOVERS!" and, of course, "RED SCUM!" Not a very edifying display for the TV cameras. Our tiny gang of four up front, separated from the remainder of the few hostile public to have gained admission wasn't ignorant to the danger to which we were exposed. But we were aware that the nazis were exercising restraint, awaiting the speech of their Fuhrer, John Tyndall.

The meeting having been sufficiently warmed-up for everyone present, it was now, indeed time for the great man to speak. The apes began to chant in unison, "TYNDALL! TYNDALL! TYNDALL!" The shabby headmaster type who answered to this name sprang up from amongst the motley collection seated around the platform. Without a moment's hesitation the apes arose as one cheering, "LEADER! LEADER!" Despite all the tension, it all began to seem mildly ludicrous. Like they'd called a Nuremberg Rally but only a few hundred had shown up. JT however was impressive in his delivery if nothing else, a seasoned demagogue. Economically gesticulating, he barked into the microphone, "THE UNIVERSITIES, THE MEDIA, THE BBC ARE RIDDLED WITH COMMUNISM!" The apes were in a state of near-religious ecstasy, "... AND

WHEN WE COME TO POWER, WE SHALL SWEEP RABBLE LIKE THIS BACK INTO THE GUTTER WHERE THEY BELONG!" Momentarily stunned into dead silence by this impressive, if slightly absurd onslaught, we counter-blasted on a level they well understood, "BOLLOCKS!" chanting "WHAT A LOAD OF RUBBISH!" Someone threw a bottle from the rear. Missing the Fuhrer by a mile, it shattered amongst the previous speakers. Then, as a block, the enraged apes arose and in a mass heaved themselves towards us, stewards barely able to exercise control. Chairs were being thrown at the rear, fists flew, the rest of the hecklers left in a body. Those of us up front now realised how detached we'd become from the main group. No time for the luxury of fear, we retreated to the main exit, spitting defiance, the stewards almost overwhelmed by enraged übers. One ape of massive dimensions threw himself into the retreating antis. A chair made little impact on his bulky frame. He went berserk, making contact more with struggling stewards than with the hated reds. Police now poured into the hall, only to be sucked into the mêlée. The opposition had vanished through the exit, leaving myself, Big Nose, Gaz, and a couple of others to slip away in all the confusion, out of the hall and into the corridor. Back inside, the tin-pot Hitler had resumed his speech, but for us it was a case of frying pan to fire. Now we were alone, surrounded by door security numbering twenty odd. The situation didn't look too healthy as a solid wall of the muscle-flexing NF heavy mob greeted us.

We pressed on undaunted until we were eyeball to eyeball. One grunted, "You lot had better watch out. There's hundreds of reds out there."

"Yeah, thanks for the tip-off, mate," I replied, for once relieved by their bone-headed stupidity.

We stepped out, into the night. Outside, protected by police lines, we found ourselves roundly abused, "NAZI SCUM! NAZI SCUM!" Such ignominy! We were all elated, however, shook hands with the asian geezer who'd slipped out with us undetected, all of us laughing at the irony of it all, and thence to the pub. We regaled everyone present with our tales of the journey into the belly of the beast. This was an experience we'd be unwilling to repeat. But our survival was the occasion for much merriment and many drinks. Outside the chanting continued. But nothing else happened that evening, racket aside.

CHAPTER 23

The next day it was off to Leicester for the National Front march. After the previous night's entertainment I was a touch fuzzy about the gills. Travelling alone, a tribute to my dedication or stupidity, I'd arranged to meet up with some mates in a pub next to the station. I kept an eye out for nazis on the train as I didn't fancy an undignified exit at sixty miles an hour. A quiet journey and a few cups of coffee saw me fresh and revitalised, however. I met up with some fellow anti-fascist enthusiasts, all eager for aggro. This crew were all known to me from past excursions apart from a total nutter in a cowboy hat who seemed ready to kick off there and then.

Things didn't look too good. Thousands of police had been deployed, making it impossible to get anywhere near the Front. So, in small groups the anti-fascists attempted as instinct dictated, to manoeuvre around the police lines, only to be restrained and pushed back by superior numbers. Cowboy Hat was a one man riot, pelting the cops with anything that came to hand. For most of the afternoon, a game of cat and mouse, along with the inevitable rumours and wild goose chases played itself out on the unremarkable streets of this Midlands town. We met up with others, tried breaking through, were forced into long diversions. All to no avail. Finally we met up in a park. Here a large crowd had gathered. Many like us had been beaten back by aggressive police kitted out with shields and handy with the batons. According to locals, the only realistic way through to the Front was via the university campus. So we upped stakes and moved on, many of us armed with rocks, bottles and other ammo. In the grounds of the university the police charged, lashing out indiscriminately with truncheons, hitting anybody within range. We now found ourselves faced with a line of police, crouching behind their long shields, knots of tooled up cops standing on the sidelines, ready for the fray. Pulling improvised masks over our faces, as did Cowboy Hat although he didn't bother to remove his distinctive headgear, we advanced on the police lines. We pelted the tooled-up cops who, unprotected by shields got a right plastering. Down they went, under a well-aimed hail, retreating, dragging a couple of their injured colleagues. This steeled us further and we bombarded the shields. They tried to advance, but were forced to pull back a few yards under the concrete confetti. Myself, Cowboy Hat and a few other headcases pushed forwards, half bricks flying over our heads, thudding against the shields. Against the stark backdrop of modernist campus buildings the two armies faced each other, like a scene from Roman times. But this time the Romans had no cavalry so it would prove difficult to disperse us. A man nudged my elbow, "Mart, is that you?" From behind his scarf I recognised a well-known aggro merchant from many past encounters. Bizarrely, as missiles rained down, lobbing our own offerings of regards, we struck up conversation about the forthcoming May Day demo in Paris. Was I going? "Yeah, staying over for a couple of days, could be fun." After the initial impact, police lines held. "A couple of dozen petrol bombs would push 'em right back!" shouted Cowboy Hat. None were forthcoming. This was, after all, England. My arm and shoulder ached from the amount of stuff I'd chucked. I fancied a change of routine. It came as, without warning, the police unleashed dogs. Out they bounded from behind the shield wall. Everyone panicked, ran off. Big mistake, the dogs brought down several unfortunates, snarling, growling, tugging at the bodies. One of the victims was female, she screamed in pain and fear. The dogs were in a frenzy, you'd have to have killed them to prevent further damage. The police followed up the dogs and charged. We pulled back. Then they sent through a couple of vans, which we stoned causing them to retreat.

We finally drifted away towards pubs, transport and home, cursing the effective policing. At the train station I met another enthusiast who seemed to be in an altogether different mood, elated. "Where were you and your mates? We had the Front, ambushed the fuckers, bricked their march, ripped 'em to shreds!" I felt jealous, even though by British standards I'd had a good day. There was, next on the agenda, the big NF meeting in Southall on Monday, only a couple of days away. We hid behind newspapers on the journey back. I noticed a couple of battered nazis. No drama though. Both sides were knackered and cops were roaming the corridors.

CHAPTER 24

It had certainly been an exhausting weekend. But Monday 23rd of April promised to be more than interesting as the Front were due to hold another Nuremberg rally in Southall Town Hall. I knew this town intimately, having a few dodgy mates round there who punted cheap blow. I also enjoyed eating out in the local curry-houses and shopping for weird, cheap prezzies from the Indian sub-continent. After a day's work, I dashed down to Paddington, catching the suburban train. I'd arranged to meet people outside the Town Hall at seven, secure entry and raise merry hell like the previous Friday.

It had been a damp wet day, and evening was drawing in as I arrived. As soon as I'd climbed the station steps, I'd become aware that something serious had already happened. We'd stand no chance of reaching the town hall as the police had blocked off the entrance to Broadway via South Street. So it looked best to try going in a westerly direction, through the back streets. A large number of people were assembled, mostly asian youth of both sexes. The mood was grim. Talking with the animated youngsters and the odd white anti-fascist acquaintance, it transpired that the cops had been having a right old beano. Apart from sealing off the town centre with several thousand foot, mounted and SPG, the whole brass band, there'd been clashes. People had been beaten up by the police, and subjected to racial abuse, arbitrary arrests, even buildings had been trashed by the uniforms. Seems there had been nothing short of a police riot that afternoon. Up until now we'd nearly always run rings around the old bill, but today it looked as though they were up for some backdated collective vengeance; not that the fuckers needed much of an excuse to kick-off in a place like Southall. An effort was being made to reach the Town Hall by about a thousand angry people, but once more, the cops were operating Roman-style, advancing slowly behind a wall of long riot shields. I could hear the odd window going in, screams, shouts, the remorseless clunk of batons against shields and the distant sound of horses' hooves. In the gathering gloom the scene was ominous to say the least.

I joined forces with a couple of Redskins and some older local geezers. More stories, dispatches from the front line. Police going berserk, heads caved in, racist taunts, brutal arrests and more. Tempers were high, no one here was cowering in fear. It was obvious there would be another serious flare-up soon. Me and the Redskins walked towards the source of the noise, more out of curiosity than any desire to plunge immediately into battle. We didn't get far due to the density of the crowds, finding ourselves standing opposite a strangely ignored, empty, yet undamaged police bus. The drizzle had yet to let up and we were thinking about take-aways when, without warning, the inevitable incident. An inconsequential looking middle aged asian man, standing next to us, pulled out from under his raincoat an unlit petrol bomb, calmly lit the fuse, tossing the flaming object. It landed directly on the vehicle roof, the instant blaze illuminating the early evening dusk. The bus skidded off, roof in flames towards the advancing police lines, the driver not caring if any of the crowd were crushed under its wheels.

The mood changed instantly, loud cheers ringing out as people fell back awaiting police retaliation. We all stood on both sides of the High Street, ammunition at the ready, with everybody young asian women included, tooled up, ready. We didn't have to wait long for the police vans to come racing through. Bricks, stones, bottles flew in abundance, smashing off the sides of the vans which didn't halt, driving off elsewhere. Our unfortunate formation ensured that many missiles intended for the cops hit members of the crowd. I was hit myself, sustaining a painful glancing blow from a rock that hit my lower leg. Nothing to worry about though, the real cause of concern being the coming police charge, possibly spearheaded by vehicles. What to do? Animated debate ensued between myself, the Redskins and a couple of SWP social worker types. We advised them to cross the road or face being trapped. But they didn't want to know. In fact they regarded us with haughty disdain, one of them in typical lisping tones calling us 'provocateurs'. Middle-class, lefty arseholes. "Fuck 'em," we thought as we manoeuvred the speeding police vehicles, reaching the other side just in time as SPG vans roared forwards in a speeding convoy. More bricks and stones flew. Some of the vans drew to a screeching halt, disgorging enraged pigs, truncheons at the ready. They piled in like maniacs, cracking skulls, sticking in the size tens, shouting and swearing their heads off. We'd made a wise choice, finding ourselves as predicted on the side opposite the drama. More vans, more pigs. With no ammo left, me and the Redskins held back. You can't take on those bastards in such circumstances, unless you fancy a kicking'n'nicking. Our minds were made up for us when a group of SPG ran towards us howling, "WE'RE 'AVIN' YOU!" "FUCKIN' PAKI LOVING CUNTS!" We fled, pursued by out of control pigs. More vans sped in, so we ducked down alleys, clambered over garden fences until we shook off the raging bloodhounds. Anyone foolish enough to dawdle was whacked, booted and if very unlucky, heaved into the back of a van. Our throats were parched, chests wheezing from exertion but we made it to safety. After a monstrous circumnavigation, we arrived back at the railway station. Adrenaline was still running high as we met more anti-nazis. We were all glad to be safe, out of it. Someone related a tale of some stray nazi getting thrown over the railway bridge onto the tracks below. "Well that's service for you," sneered one of the Redskins. We all laughed.

Next day the papers were full of it, "RIOT!" "POLICE SEEK OUTSIDE AGITATORS!" Nothing about the Front or the bussed-in police, few of whom were exactly indigenous to the area. More importantly, there had been a tragic death. The police had killed an ANL member named Blair Peach with a blow to the head in Beechcroft Avenue. Was he amongst the group who'd regarded us with such disdain, refusing to cross the road, ending up trapped? Hundreds were dragged though the courts on trumped-up charges, heavy sentences resulted and of course not one copper was prosecuted. All the usual bollocks followed, government and media in happy harmony.

Not long after these events came the General Election. Thatcher was in. The grim '80s were about to start. The Front vote collapsed shortly afterwards, followed by the organisation itself that divided into factions, squabbling like rabid weasels in a sack. The Tories had stolen their thunder, puking out racist garbage by the ton. So the punters went for it, including large numbers of white working class of both genders. Stupid, ignorant cunts.

CHAPTER 25

My final clash of the decade with the Master Race proved to be one of the bloodiest of all. My interest in the übers had declined, besides you can't maintain such violent momentum forever. Not without serious injury or a spell behind bars. In spite of election results there had also been a change, albeit slight, in working class racism and support for fascists such as the NF. At least a significant minority of the younger generation had become vociferously opposed to racist garbage, they'd come into friendly contact with ethnic minorities at work, in their leisure time and of course through the ANL which for all its faults and limitations had provided an alternative to the hideous racism so sadly the norm in the sixties and throughout most of the seventies. But there was no let up in racist terror and attacks. They appeared to be becoming more deadly as electoral and street support drained from the Front. This was allied to a revival of the skinhead craze with all the attendant violent racism, 'paki bashing' in particular. Of course, not all skins were racist morons, some were anti-fascist like the Redskins hooligan firm we'd encountered at Southall. Many however were; it was part of the fashion. The Front had attracted boneheads who'd hung about on the fringes, much to the discomfort of the tweedy leadership. The group that welcomed them with open arms was the hardcore British Movement.

This last incident came about more or less by chance. One free Saturday night I was called, asked if I fancied doing door security for a benefit gig. The cause, 'Persons Unknown', an aspiring 'Angry Brigade Mk II' currently awaiting trial on terrorism charges. I said, "Sure, why not." At least I'd be spared the dreadful punk music of the band Crass who were the main star turn. The gig was being held at the scene of that fatal encounter with the police way back in 1974, Conway Hall, Red Lion Square.

The hopelessness of London Transport ensured that it took me an age to arrive. When eventually I did, an unwelcome sight greeted me. Around forty plus British Movement skinheads had barged in and were gathered inside the main entrance exuding menace. It didn't take long to evaluate the situation. Hopeless. A dozen of them were large brutes, evil looking bastards, real hardnuts, with another dozen or so inner core. The remainder were merely runty followers, but dangerous if mob-handed or tooled up. The organisation of the gig had collapsed, nazis ruled the roost. The only thing holding them back from rampage was that they were waiting for Crass to come on for the finale, then they'd rush and take the stage. (All in all, an act demanding stern courage as Crass were abject pacifists and didn't physically retaliate). As I pondered what to do next, I realised that this was our only slim advantage.

Abandoning the door, I tried to further suss out the opposition. Like the bullies they were, the boneheads were amusing themselves by insulting the punters, punks and anarcho-trendies who avoided dialogue or body contact, wise under the circumstances. The BM officer-class stood out from the foot soldiers, with extra shiny pates, many stripes decorating their pug-ugly fizzogs. Indeed, they were the most repulsive specimens of sub-humanity I believe I'd ever seen. Dressed in traditional skinhead regalia, a couple of their leaders were decked out in Crombies and Ben Shermans. The cherry-red steelies were simply itching to perform to the tune of maximum damage. Many of the others were rigged out in bomber jackets. I noticed, most intriguingly, one of them was of mixed race. Clearly a lad with some severe identity problems. But I wasn't about to wheel out the shrink's couch, I had to get something together to at least prevent this from being a walkover.

I'd managed to gather around half a dozen lads, most of whom had accompanied me on previous jaunts, could be depended on, and were willing to have a proper go. The trendy anarcho-types were no good in a fight, unless of course, it involved the missus. Besides, they were always hinting, if not stating outright that there was only a marginal difference between us anti-fascists and the nazis themselves. Now faced with such a raw situation, no longer able to afford the luxury of such pontificating, they kept their traps shut.

I was called over to the door, asked to step outside; someone had been enquiring after me by name. Curious, I stepped out into the chill October night to be met by a couple of anti-fascists who were attached to the SWP. I'd joined these characters on many a past expedition against the Master Race. Someone had been on the blower as these lads had everything well-sussed. "Can you keep the lid on it for a couple of hours? We're gonna get our crew together, steam 'em real heavy ... if, of course, you don't mind."

"It'll be difficult," I mused, "But I'll do my best. I know they're waiting for Crass to go on so they can storm the stage. Crass are headlining, so they won't be on till last."

"You and your mates don't mind us having the bastards knowing that Crass won't get to play?"

"Far as I'm concerned," I retorted, "This gig's been fucked from the beginning. I don't give a monkey's what people think so long as these nazi fuckers get what's coming to 'em. Anyway, you'll be doing my eardrums a favour. I can't stand this racket."

They departed for the warmth of a nearby pub. "We'll send word when we're ready. See you outside."

The SWP, scared of losing control of some of their more volatile, plebeian supporters who really believed in smashing the fascists, had never warmed to this semi-clandestine group. Maybe because these people were ready to link up on the day with anybody on the left, anarchists or anti-fascists who were willing to have a crack at the NF or BM heavies. They'd proved themselves time and again, and I preferred their direct attitude to that of the trendy wankers of the anarchist movement who condemned such behaviour as 'macho'. Boring, dull, middle class snobs.

I communicated the plan to my half-dozen confidantes. They seemed well pleased. Our main task was to dampen things down, ensure it didn't kick off to our disfavour before the appointed time, stop the BM from beating-up and rolling punters in isolated corners. It would be difficult. Within ten minutes word arrived of trouble in the main hall, so in we walked, amidst the migrane-inducing punk noise to see a knot of BM menacing a couple of spiky-hairs. Throwing all caution to the wind, I strode over, separated them from their tormentors and escorted the punks to another part of the building. Naturally, I felt nervous, worried to the extreme. I didn't fancy a kicking, much less a premature free-for-all in which we'd be massacred. The skins were annoyed at the intervention, pissed-off by my diplomacy as I shunted the punks away to safety. I didn't get an instant pounding so I guessed I'd been correct to assume that the nazis were saving their aggro for a pre-arranged storming of the stage.

After a short breather, I was summoned to the bogs, and it wasn't for a closet assignation in a cubicle. "It's real trouble, want us to come with you?"

I declined. If we arrived mob-handed, it would kick off. This I didn't want. "Just wait at the bottom of the stairs. If you hear a big row, come and get me out if you can. If you can't then I'll see you in hospital."

Up the stairs I went, opening the door to be confronted by the sight of one of their leaders and half a dozen crew pinning a young asian lad against the wall. "Don't fuckin' argue you FUCKIN' PAKI CUNT, just give us your money CUNT!" I didn't have the time to dash and collect an anti-sexist to correct this fellow's patriarchal attitude. I'd clocked this evil looking brute before, he looked the part, shaven skull, vile white eyebrows, tramlines, psycho eyes. The light reflected off the collected ping-pong heads. No time for fear or anything I plunged in, grabbing the asian lad. "Right you! Making trouble again? Winding these geezers up are we?" I yanked him out from the astounded group, one of whom I'd notice fingering a small blade.

"Oi! What's your fuckin' game?" snarled their leader.

"Security!" I'd managed to extricate the trembling lad to the point of getting as far as the door when a couple more skins entered, opening the door. This allowed me to bundle the lad upstairs.

"Sorry mate," I apologised, "Really sorry about that, sorry about the whole fucking night. Hope you understand." He did. I remarked. "It's a bit like being back at school innit?"

"Yeah, too right guv," he laughed nervously. I advised him to, "Fuck off or find your mates."

"I was going to meet friends here," he said, "But they haven't shown up yet."

I reassured him, "Look mate, I shouldn't be telling you this, but there's gonna be some right heavy geezers coming here later to sort this lot out. I'm just trying to keep the lid on things." He took the message and headed home.

An hour to go. Could it be contained? Would the heavy mob show? No time to fret, another incident, this time in the corridor. Same bastard with the albino orangutang eyebrows, same tactics from me, except I had a couple of geezers standing handy in the background. On this occasion they were picking on a geeky-fellow with specs. Or rather who had been wearing glasses, as they were now being ground down under the size-ten cherry reds of the leader who spat into the face of his victim. "I don't like cunts with Anti-Nazi League badges, you FUCKIN' RED QUEERBOY!"

"He ain't no red, just another fuckin troublemaker who doesn't know when he's not welcome," I said, strolling in to snatch the geek.

White eyebrows wasn't having any of it. "I'm getting sick and tired of you butting in, CUNT!"

He didn't lay hands on me, but stood eyeball to eyeball. Just to add to my discomfort his breath didn't exactly smell of roses. I backed down, refusing to match his aggressive body-language. A large crowd had gathered, taking advantage, I managed to spirit the unhappy geek away, followed by white eyebrows mouthing obscenities: "CUNT! I'm gonna slash you up good an' fuckin' proper. Do you hear me? CUNT!" Again, none of the anti-sexists stepped forward to admonish him for his language. Wonder why? By now, this catalogue of incidents had me seething with suppressed anger, fear, frustration, humiliation. At least Eyebrows hadn't followed up his threats, as he goose-stepped with his crew into yet another drama.

Time certainly didn't pass quickly as one incident followed another. The gig was going full blast as intimidation was played out in the recesses. Most of the anarchos were in the main concourse, gathered in small groups, looking worried. Apart from the half dozen I'd collected who were tried, tested, willing to have a go, the rest were next to useless. Besides, having endured years of criticism for alleged 'macho bully boy tactics' when it came to dealing with the nazis I knew I couldn't trust that bunch with anything. One of their chicks, who under normal circumstances couldn't bring herself to speak to me without a prize sneer handed me an iron bar she'd found somewhere. Such generosity. I wasn't impressed, "What do I want that for?" I asked. "Look, I'm already tooled up," pointing to the trusty crowbar tucked down my pants. "Why don't you give it to one of your men? Don't take much to bop some nazi on the head does it?" She looked at me with a mixture of incomprehension and disgust.

After an eternity, a message from the pub: "Get your lads outside in five minutes, we'll all pile in together." At last. Just in time too, as the skins were massing in the concourse prior to rushing the stage. I'd even had a friendly reminder from Eyebrows: "I'm gonna have you myself, later, CUNT!" With Preston, our main nutter, we slipped outside to be met by the other anti-fascists. Here stood a mixture of Cockney Reds in Manchester United scarves and other trusted nutters I knew, meaner looking than most of the thugs inside the hall, and older geezers in no mood for compromise.

"This all you've got?" one of them asked.

"Yeah," I replied, ashamed of the piss-poor turnout. "But don't worry, we'll have a real go. I've got a score to settle, some blonde headed cunt." I brandished a broken bottle in one hand, crowbar in another.

"Yeah haven't we all," retorted another voice.

I noticed they were all tooled up and numbered just over a dozen.

"How many, where are they?"

"Forty maybe, some tasty, but most will run. One's got a blade, the rest I don't know, but I haven't seen anything." I told them the majority were now in the concourse.

"Good, well done for keeping it all together...IT's PARTY TIME!!!." And with that we all crashed through the doors.

One unlucky bystander who didn't shift himself quickly enough was the first to suffer, a bottle smashed over his head. Screams of horror went up from the girls, whilst the brave anarcho men fled, or stood rooted to the spot in a state of shock. They hadn't been warned of the impending floorshow. We hurled ourselves straight into the main body who scattered and ran. Eyebrows and all the hard nuts stood their ground, all to no avail. We were on them, no pity. Me and Preston smashed out bottles into Eyebrows' head, more tramlines for his collection. Then as Preston jabbed him in the face with the bottle neck, I struck his head with blows from the crowbar. He hit the deck, blood pouring. He then had the pleasure of tasting our boots as we dished out size ten vengeance, kicking his head to a pulp. All around, utter mayhem as bottles flew, crashing into walls, whilst the nazis struggled desperately as they were overwhelmed by a storm of steel capped boots, iron bars, chains, knives, broken bottles. The whole area filled with screams, yells, hundreds of panic-stricken punters tried to flee past the battle scene. Within a minute a heap of semi-conscious bodies lay where they'd fallen, blood splattered on the walls, pools of claret leaking in steady trickles onto the floor. Some nazis were trying to crawl under chairs and tables to escape the kicks of those they'd previously scorned and terrorised. Payback time. By now, the novocaine tingle had frozen my upper lip; the classic adrenaline rush. We split into small groups, chasing the nazis into the main hall and corridors. The übers fled in all directions, leaving them vulnerable to our frenzied attack. We smashed them into a pulp; iron bars smacking into heads and bodies. No mercy was shown as we hunted down the heavies, the foot soldiers hurriedly discarding nazi insignia and badges, running for cover. In all the confusion, violence, yells and cries, I noticed the mixed-race geezer ripping off his badge and disappearing out the doors. I let him be. Someone had to live to tell the tale, spread the word to the others. Down the corridor, contrary to fire regulations, the exit doors were bolted shut. A handful of skins rattled the doors, trying to escape. All in vain. Down they went, set upon by the anti-nazis who beat crap out of them. Resistance was useless as they were kicked to fuck. A glorious end to the night. The British Movement Heavy Mob, stormtroopers of the master-race, bloody and battered.

Preston grabbed me, "Come on, let's split." Reluctantly, I drew back, my coat flecked with blood, shards of glass gleaming from elbow to hands. We backed out of the corridor. Skins were on their knees, pleading for mercy in the chaos as anti-nazi nutters stood over them, blades drawn. Some of the younger more pathetic nazis were spared cold steel, although all got a good slapping. Other were stabbed and slashed. Nothing fatal, but a life-long reminder of that night's encounter and the error of their ways. Did I have an ounce of pity, sorrow or remorse for the brutality that unfolded before me? Did I fuck! The battle in the main hall must have been ferocious for in the dim light I saw prostrate bodies, smashed furniture and a deserted stage. Looked like the gig was off. We both headed for the main exit past a few anarcho drones who were still frozen to the spot as if in a horrified trance. I passed one of the women who'd been a regular tormentor. "Remember you said we were as bad as the nazis? Well it ain't true... we're fuckin' worse! Goodnight darlin'." Then out into the night. We'd suffered no casualties apart from a few superficial cuts and bruises. We dumped our tools in the surrounding streets. Lucky it had been a chill autumn otherwise we'd have left behind our dabs. As it was, most of us had been wearing gloves. Police vans drew up. The cops must have been greeted by utter devastation as they entered the hall. We'd all fucked off by then, happy as Larry, some home, others to distant pubs. Never content, even with a crushing victory, some legged it to the tube hoping to pick off the stragglers. I was home a couple of hours later, the phone ringing constantly, my refrain, "You've missed a good one tonight..." I suppose in my heart of hearts the reaction following the Conway Hall bloodbath didn't really surprise me, although I was taken aback for a while. After years of abuse, insults and cold-shouldering from many in the anarcho scene, it came as no great shock. Even so, it infuriated me. The group Crass and their support band the Poison Girls, issued weighty statements. There were shock horror reports of the carnage in *The Guardian* and *Time Out*. The BM nazis were treated as sacrificial lambs, despite them outnumbering us over two to one. We and our friends from the left were 'Red Fascists' a 'Football Gang', 'their leaders appeared to be Scots', even in the supposedly Liberal press of the day a by-word for 'nutter'. Such parochialism. Even the nazis would blush. The odium was heaped on me and others, but I withstood it with the usual fortitude, a couple of minor outbursts aside. After all, my critics would soon disappear into the halls of academia, respectability, the Labour Party, the media and property-owning classes. Fuck 'em. The urban riots of the '80s were just around the corner and I was still young and ready to ruck, no burnout for me.

It had been an interesting decade, the Seventies, and I think I'd contributed to the overall pattern of increasing violence. An even more violent, more turbulent time lay ahead. But that, as they say, is another story.